Real Estate v2.0

Also by Danielle Babb

Commissions at Risk: A Real Estate Professional's
Guide to Beating Online Competition

Finding Foreclosures: An Insider's Guide to
Cashing In on This Hidden Market

Make Money Teaching Online:
How to Land Your First Academic Job,
Build Credibility, and Earn a Six-Figure Salary

Real Estate v2.0

A Professional's Guide to Dynamic Websites, Blogs, and Podcasts

Danielle Babb, PhD, MBA
and Alex Lazo, PhD, MS

KAPLAN

PUBLISHING

New York

This publication is designed to provide accurate and authoritative information in regard to the subject matter covered. It is sold with the understanding that the publisher is not engaged in rendering legal, accounting, or other professional service. If legal advice or other expert assistance is required, the services of a competent professional should be sought.

Vice President and Publisher: Maureen McMahon
Editorial Director: Jennifer Farthing
Acquisitions Editor: Michael Sprague
Development Editor: Joshua Martino
Production Editor: Julio Espin
Production Designer: Todd Bowman
Cover Designer: Rod Hernandez

Published by Kaplan Publishing, a division of Kaplan, Inc.
1 Liberty Plaza
New York, NY 10006

978-1-4277-9596-0

Printed in the United States of America

2007   10 9 8 7 6 5 4 3 2 1

Kaplan Publishing books are available at special quantity discounts to use for sales promotions, employee premiums, or educational purposes. Please email our Special Sales Department to order or for more information at *kaplanpublishing@ kaplan.com,* or write to Kaplan Publishing, 1 Liberty Plaza, 24th Floor, New York, NY 10006.

Dedications

This book is dedicated to my grandfather Bill.
May your memory live forever in our hearts
and your soul in Heaven with the Lord.

DANI BABB

I dedicate this book to my wife and kids,
my parents, and my brother.

ALEX LAZO

Contents

Foreword

THE HOUSING INDUSTRY touches every household in the United States, affects most of the nation's developed real estate, and is responsible for trillions of dollars in annual business transactions. Despite this vast economic and social impact, the industry has always been slow to adapt to new technology, especially in the Internet age. Not content to leave housing professionals behind in the 20th century, Dani Babb and Alex Lazo have given us this highly illuminating yet succinct guide to leverage Internet tools that are both accessible and user friendly.

The authors focus on the sale of real estate by brokers, but this is only the starting point for the educational value of this book. Their presentation of effective Internet tools for finding, displaying, and selling real estate for buyers and sellers is equally applicable to marketing multifamily rental housing and other commercial real estate. With major real estate brokers moving from print media to online marketing, other housing professionals will have no choice but to follow.

As with most Internet technology, one must understand what an online tool can do before using it. Ms. Babb and Mr. Lazo bring complex understanding to the reader in a most palatable form. The mysteries of dynamic websites, blogs, podcasts, and domain marketing are unlocked for all to see.

KERRY W. KIRBY
Chief Executive Officer, 365 Connect
Founder and Publisher, MultifamilyBiz.com

Introduction

Introduction to Using Dynamic Websites, Blogs, and Podcasts in Real Estate

Technology has a profound impact on just about every industry. While service sectors used to be somewhat immune (commodities and products were first to become webified), the Web is taking hold in many service markets—real estate included. Many in the real estate profession object to the notion that transactions could be conducted without their direct expertise. We agree that technology cannot do everything—technology does not know your market and cannot hold an open house, for instance. Technology cannot provide human contact the way you, the real estate professional, can.

As technologists, however, we know that more and more people expect to do things quickly online. They want information online, and they want websites to be intuitive and know what they want without their having to ask for it. They want a community to visit, not just a website that sends information that they request. They want user-generated content, and they want dynamic, entertaining information. They want you to educate them, and they want you to provide useful information. They want it all integrated and aggregated, and they want you, the real estate professional, to provide it—at no cost to them!

In this book, we are going to tell you how to do it all using three small steps. As a real estate professional, you have an opportunity to integrate your work into the Internet via dynamic, customer-driven Web 2.0 sites that offer value and insight.

So Why Technology and Real Estate, and Why Now?

Newspapers, magazines, and TV news reveal the trend towards information technology's changing every industry. In the 1990s, companies like E*Trade Financial revolutionized the way that individuals and experienced investors alike traded stocks. Consumers were suddenly given information and analysis previously available only to investors or brokers. We saw buyers and sellers interacting directly under "perfect market" conditions using tools like eBay, and we saw eToys take a strong hold over other toy companies' market shares. Amazon.com changed the book world forever.

We saw travel agents lose their jobs as companies like Expedia and Travelocity became ubiquitous. Call centers in India pop up for pennies on the dollar to handle routine travel booking transactions through websites offering value-added service, like direct hotel communication and hotel research, 24/7 support, and reduced costs.

Even in high-end retail, where "service is king," brick-and-mortar stores are being replaced quickly by online e-tailers offering great service at a lower price, often with no sales tax, no shipping fee, and even free return shipping. Smart retailers are realizing this and providing their own high-end products online through high-end e-tailers like eLuxury, and others are consolidating or buying one another in hopes of surviving.

Right before our eyes, Voice over Internet Protocol (VoIP) companies like Skype and Vonage are taking over traditional telecommunications provided by giant organizations by finding better methods and replacing existing technology with consumer-friendly, inexpensive alternatives. They, in turn, get purchased by big companies like eBay.

The Web has also changed the real estate industry for good. Online companies are offering low-cost and flat-fee full-service home sales. People are turning to online companies to value and list their home. Several studies report that 90 percent of real estate agents have high-speed Internet access at home, up from 82 percent in 2004 and 71 percent in 2003. For 46 percent of real estate agents, email is their primary method of communication with clients, and 31 percent noted that their most important technology upgrades in 2005 were handheld devices that allowed them to retrieve email remotely (Newton 2005). Sixty percent of real estate agents post listings to their own websites, and 67 percent view the Internet as extremely or very important in the marketing and promotion of their sales. This survey revealed that 33 percent of business comes from the Internet. Of individuals who look for homes, 80 percent use the Internet in their search, and that number is increasing every day. Some estimates put it at over 90 percent!

Take a look at how the industry has changed in a little over ten years. Compare the Internet-driven real estate world to the ten-decade-old MLS, and you can immediately see the impact of the Internet revolution. In 1995, only 2 percent of homebuyers used the Internet as a source of information. In 1997, this rose to 18 percent. In 1999, this more than doubled to 37 percent. In 2003, the number rose to over 40 percent. Now Internet researchers are at over 80 percent and growing. The Internet is a tremendous value for homebuyers and investors who are looking to find, purchase, and rent property with ease. Investors have been finding new areas and properties online for years.

Today, the Internet is enabling real estate professionals and their associated transactions—for the better. Technology is a real estate professional's good friend—a way to market quickly, to create immeasurable market share and visibility, and most certainly to grasp a competitive advantage by those who use it to the fullest. Lots of new technologies, many discussed in this book, can help you get a handle on the future. Learning about emerging technologies will help you continue your success in the real estate marketplace.

1 An Overview of Real Estate Technology

AS A REAL estate professional, you know that if you're going to provide technology and services online, you need to understand how they work. Thanks to a flurry of new tools for people who want to push their incredible work out to the public, you don't need to be a technical expert. But you should have a solid understanding of available technology and how it has changed in the last three years. Before we show you how to use podcasts, blogs, and dynamic websites in your business, we'll explain—using little technical jargon—what they are and what they mean for your business.

What Is "New Media"?

The cutting-edge Web technology that we will discuss in this book is known as the "New Media." *New Media* is what we use and see every day on the Web—sites like MySpace and YouTube. This term encompasses many types of media. Here is a list of some of them (Rumford 2006). Note that we have provided a list of key terms and definitions in Appendix A, where we describe how these terms apply to you, the real estate pro.

- *Audio podcasting.* You may wish to advertise about your services or about your business.
- *Video podcasting.* You may wish to showcase homes or offer informative seminars.
- *Blogging.* You may wish to blog about a market, a method, or why others should know you are *the* expert.
- *Video blogging (vlog).* You might want to create infomercials or seminars for your clients.
- *Video sharing.* This is a great way to build your network base.
- *Social networking.* Here's another networking tool, but it will include not only other experts but potential and existing clients.
- *Social bookmarking.* You want to be the go-to person!
- *Wiki.* Explain terminology and concepts that others may not—making you the expert.
- *RSS.* This is a way to get your information out there.
- *XML.* This development methodology makes for a great site.
- *Mobile social networks.* Let people connect with you from the most remote of places.

You may not know what all of these terms mean yet, but as you read on, you'll discover why these terms are relevant both to your business and the industry as a whole.

What Is Web Version 2?

First, we will explain the premise behind all of these technologies: Web version 2.0, commonly referred to as "Web v2." This somewhat vague term means relying on user-generated content to create dynamic sites. The fantastic websites that allow you to customize the page, become a part of a network of users, post your thoughts, save your favorites, link to other "friends" and post just about anything you like—these are all part of Web v2! Simply put, Web v2 refers to online content produced by users of a website rather than by the traditional method, in which someone who works for a company or a marketing group displays specific information with a specific purpose. Rather than pushing information out to clients, there is reciprocity in Web v2—people share.

Wikipedia, YouTube, and MySpace.com are examples of user-generated sites that are quite popular. You can see quickly how they differ from sites that aim to push specific news or information on their site visitors. Web v2 sites allow ordinary people to publish their own content online. This method has given the average Internet user a new perspective and control over Web content. In fact, user-generated content is creating fame and fortune for people who may not otherwise have had access to media outlets. Have you heard of Lonelygirl15 on YouTube? If you do a Google search, you will undoubtedly learn all about this aspiring actress's use of YouTube to create a following, if not a career.

She isn't the only one. Companies are putting profiles online for their products! Users of MySpace can become a "friend" to the Whopper hamburger. Why is this important? The younger generations, who live and breathe this technology, are identifying themselves and quantifying their personality by who they befriend. As a result, tech-savvy businesspeople are using the medium to get the word out about themselves and their products to a whole new generation of people. For you, this means first-time homebuyers and investors.

Why Is Everything Changing? Why Fix What Isn't Broken?

In the past, information sources have been unidirectional, even in the real estate market. That is, there has been a clear provider of information and an equally clear recipient. You went to a TV channel, newspaper, magazine, or book and requested information that was presented to you. Or, in the case of the "early Web," you went to the website and just took whatever the site creators gave you.

Television contains a vast array of information that users cannot control beyond changing the channel. Viewers are completely passive when we watch. (Sure, some of you might yell at the screen, but that's not what we mean!) The TV displays the emitted signal, which terminates in our eyes and ears. Whatever *they* want you to hear is what you hear, and what they want you to see (product placement and advertisements) is done at your expense and for their revenue stream.

But what if you could push back? What if you and every other viewer could contribute to the broadcasts? Some television shows have become famous for interactivity—offering the ability to vote by phone, for instance. Why are they so successful? People feel as though their vote matters, they become engaged, and the experience becomes viral. Instead of watching some anchor deliver news that someone somewhere else has deemed relevant, you provide your own input and can be on equal footing with everyone else. Some anchors now read live email on news broadcasts! Why? To create as much interactivity as plain old television allows and compete with the dynamic Internet sites that have grabbed our attention from the television. This is the spirit of Web 2.0, best described as the "participatory Web" (Decrem 2006).

Everything You Need to Know—Without the Techie Terms!

Perhaps you can already imagine the relevance of Web v2 technology to the real estate industry. In fact, not only is this technology relevant to what you do, it is also complementary. We can already see consumer-generated information in the content-rich formats of Domania.com, innovative pricing models displayed nicely at

Zillow.com, and the incredible power that online MLS searching has brought to the average buyer. Did you ever think an online technology would "make you move"? Check out Zillow's Make Me Move feature!

What will happen to you when these consumer-oriented and user-generated sites take hold in your business—if they haven't already? Let's face it, the average consumer has access to tools that even the professionals only used to dream about. Not long ago, even the pros were going through thick books of infrequently updated data. We'll explain how to use the tools of today to their fullest and what to expect as the future of technology takes shape.

What's a Podcast?

We'll go into podcasting in more detail later in the book. For now, we want you to get a brief sense of each Web v2 technology so you can relate each technology to the others.

Podcasting has changed the way many of us use the Internet; it has changed the way we watch shows, get our news, and share our ideas. Even major television networks are making shows available via podcasting. Who hasn't heard of the Apple iPod or YouTube? Some argue that these two technologies have changed the way we do everything. The impact of Apple's portable music- and video-playing device is easy to see—it's everywhere! And you've surely heard of the notable Google buyout of famous (or infamous) YouTube. Interviews with Google such as those in *Wired* magazine indicate that Google set aside $200 million in legal fees after the buyout due to potential lawsuits—which of course happened. Google believes it's worth it because of the potential revenue for ad dollars regardless of legal costs. This is an indicator of how hot online media will be in the future; hot enough Google was willing to spend a lot of money not only for the buyout but the legal downfall afterwards. Podcasts will be front and center in the real estate Internet revolution. It will be up to you to decide how to use them to help you grow your business as you've never imagined. It isn't nearly as difficult as most people believe to get started and really grasp the technology.

A *podcast* is an audio or video file (such as an MP3 audio file) that a content provider makes available on the Internet. This file, often referred to as one episode of a podcast, can be located at a URL (a website address). Some systems let individuals subscribe to the website to be notified of new podcasts when they become available or even have them automatically downloaded to their computers. The term *podcasting* refers to the distribution of a multimedia file over the Internet through the use of syndication feeds. Playback of this file can be accomplished with a mobile device or PC. Wikipedia, the online encyclopedia, defines *podcast* as "a digital media file, or a series of such files, that is distributed over the Internet using syndication feeds for playback on portable media players and personal computers. A podcast is a specific type of webcast which, like 'radio,' can mean either the content itself or the method by which it is syndicated; the latter is also termed *podcasting*. The host or author of a podcast is often called a *podcaster.*"

If you believe that your clients won't want information from this medium, you are mistaken; they already do, and they are already getting it. You can use their adoption of this technology to your advantage. Throughout each section of this book, where we identify what to do to make the best use of technologies, we will explain how.

You can become a podcaster just by hosting your own blog or podcast. You can use inexpensive (even free) software referred to as "open source blog software." This means that people can feel free to modify it and use it as they need. Usually in the interest of sharing, you would communicate any useful and meaningful updates you make to the software to the online community. However, the hosted versions of podcasts and blogs do require that the user leave your site and go to the hosted site, which isn't always a good thing. Therefore, hosting the podcast or blog yourself is definitely worth considering, and it isn't as hard as it sounds.

One of the first websites to support blogs was *http://podblaze. com*. Podblaze founder Rodney Rumford believes that the future of podcasting and real estate are inseparable. We agree—audio tours of homes and podcasts will become the industrywide standard. Users may even find homes by using what today are already traditional podcasting search techniques. Do you want to run the risk of not finding the perfect buyer for a home you are selling because you didn't podcast it? Or because you didn't offer enough information about you and/or your business up front? This would be an obvious mistake—one that we don't want you to make.

Some believe that podcasting is "overmarketing," but it isn't—not in today's Internet age. While over 80 percent of people look for homes today online, how they look is always changing. People want to be engaged, and to feel engaged, they need to use more powerful means than traditional virtual tours and picture shows. The goal is, first, to make sure any potential buyer will look at a house you are selling and, second, to attract new potential buyers. Podcasts can help you do both.

A big advantage of podcasts for a home seller is that they provide potential buyers with the opportunity to preview the home thoroughly prior to setting foot in it. They eliminate the odd view that virtual tours give, and they incorporate sound via audio clips from the seller and the agent and just about anything else you can dream up. Using podcasts can eliminate some of the looky-loos that eat up your time (like neighbors browsing homes to see what the Joneses had in that living room). More importantly, it will help ensure that those who enter the home already have some minimal level of interest in it. Nothing is more frustrating for sellers than to go through the hassle of tidying up their home in preparation for a showing, only to have the viewers take two steps into the house, then turn around and leave because of some glaring negative. A podcast allows potential buyers to see the feature and change their minds—without going near the house.

Podcasts Are Sprucing Up Traditional Business

So what are some other uses for podcasts? University lectures, news broadcasts, political campaigns, tours of cities, newspapers, advocacy, law enforcement crime watch, live music streams, events, advertisements, screencasting (teaching us how to use a computer)—you name it, and it's out there! The great thing about podcasting is that it is easy—even for someone who isn't exactly computer savvy.

Podcasts are an example of a technology that has achieved a state of ubiquity due to dramatic increases in data transfer rates. A few years ago, most of us gained access to the Internet via dial-up modems. Had broadband (high-speed) connectivity such as DSL and cable not become available, podcasting could have been likened to driving a high-performance sports car in city traffic. In other words, if you can't use it to its full potential, what's the point? However, the rich video and audio that podcasts normally contain can be fully enjoyed by users with only a relatively short download time. Your buyers and sellers have this technology at home, so it's in your best interest to take advantage of it.

The Newest in Podcasting

What's next for podcasts? We are starting to see a number of new uses enter the marketplace—peercasting (live streaming), vodcasting (video podcasting), mobilecasting (podcasting to mobile phones), and blogcasting (the blogging podcast). This is only the beginning; as our devices become more integrated and our bandwidth grows, resulting in faster connection speeds, New Media will go to yet another level. Think tanks and technologists in Silicon Valley are already planning it, and as real estate professionals, we need to get ready.

What Kind of Stuff Can I Podcast?

You can use podcasts to advertise in lots of ways. Most of the major news outlets actually force you to watch commercials before an online video clip. Unlike with digital video recording services like TiVo, users cannot just move past the commercials. Marketing companies are buying space on websites, and some argue that product placement will become very important even in podcasts in the future. Advertisers love podcast technology, because they can get more customer data than ever and monitor who is visiting your site and what they are doing. You will know who has viewed your material, for how long, and where they went when they left your site. You can see how long they spent reviewing different parts of your site and what pages grabbed their attention immediately. Even the television media industry isn't that specific, still relying on polls and ratings.

New technologies are creating indexes of key words used in podcast broadcasts. Many find this capability even more powerful than traditional search engines! Right now, only text is searchable. But imagine what will happen when your videocast has the words *beach property* in it (not your text, remember, but your words) and the search engine can find it! How powerful will that be? That feature is coming sooner than we think. Check out websites like *http://podzinger.com* and *http://blinkx.com*. The relevance of vodcasts is growing too. Most personal digital assistants (PDAs) and even cell phones have the ability to play videos. Technology will soon allow people, using global positioning systems (GPSs) built into devices, to identify homes for sale within a few miles of their position at any given point and see a full video of the house, complete with audio. This takes the "talking open house" to an extreme! (Take a look at "Podcasts in Real Estate—Some Examples" in Appendix B for some specific sites that you can visit.)

The Blog Bandwagon—Blogs Aren't Just for Teenagers!

Everyone seems to have a blog these days, from teens on My-Space to political commentators. There are so many blogs that without email feeds, it seems nearly impossible to stay on top of them all. How many blogs or forums have you posted to only to forget the name and never log in again? (Technology is working on a solution for that problem, too, by the way!)

So what is a blog exactly? Blog is short for *Web log*. A blog is a website where the creator makes journal-style entries. They usually provide comments on newsworthy or controversial topics or on subject matter in which people want to be educated. Some people also use them as online diaries. Usually blogs have content such as text, pictures, links, and even file sharing or other media. Blogs generally attract a particular group of people who are interested in a particular topic. Readers can leave comments in the blog, and this interactive nature is an important distinguishing element.

What are some other important elements of blogs? Knowing a few key phrases will help you as you read more about blogging. A *blogger*, for example, is someone who creates and maintains a blog. Blogs can be written for personal digital assistants (PDAs), the Web, or mobile phones (blogs for this type of medium are referred to as moblogs), and they can focus on any subject in which the blogger is interested. Once you start a blog on a particular topic, you will be amazed at how many share your concerns, your viewpoints, and your interest in the topic—and your readers will generate buzz about you and your writing. As a real estate professional, you will create a blog that has something to do with real estate in a content area in which both you and your audience are interested.

Some search engines are dedicated to blogs, and you can also search specifically for blog topics in the major general search engines. Most blogs don't generate revenue, but some people have gotten creative with banner ads, donations, or sponsorships. Even "click to donate" models have been made popular by political bloggers.

Elements of Blogs

A blog has several elements, each making the blog unique and identifiable to the blogging community and to the individuals that work on the blog. One element is the title, which is the headline of the post. Next comes the body of the blog post, which contains the content you want viewers to read. This "push" element of blogs is much like that of traditional media. Where it differs is in the response—the interactivity that occurs after you make your blog entry. The URL or the permalink is the full article that you want to display. The post includes its date and time, and it may optionally include comments, categories, and/or TrackBacks that refer to the original entry (Wikipedia, "Blog," 2006). Blogs are often seen as a way for nonmainstream persons to get around the "filter" that exists in mainstream media. Recently, mainstreamers have joined the blogosphere (the community of blogs and bloggers) as well, creating blogs themselves. A published blog software comparison chart available at the University of Southern California's *Online Journalism Review* (*www.ojr.org/ojr/images/ blog_software_comparison.cfm*) shows lots of options for bloggers to host and maintain their Web logs.

Blogs are a great way to market your expertise and your services. If nothing else, you should host a blog on your site with weekly updates and let other people respond, generating some buzz on your area of expertise and your topic. This is a good feedback loop by which to understand your visitors' thoughts and interests. It's also a good way to attract other professionals to your site who may have business for you or with whom you may be able to partner. In fact, the term *blog marketing* is receiving much hype nowadays, and advertisers are paying attention. One site that you might want to look at is *http://realestateblogmarketing.com*. It provides lots of helpful advice for real estate professionals who want to use blogs.

One of your goals is to increase traffic and sales from your website, and your blog is one of many ways to accomplish that. You want to be sure that you establish yourself as an expert, first and foremost, regardless of how casual or formal your blog. You need to use your blog to differentiate yourself from your competition, and you need to be an authority on your topic. People will respect you and will value your opinions. You can also make it clear to the world that you embrace, rather than reject or feel threatened by, technology! Blogs are relatively new phenomena used by businesses, and they are even more innovative in the real estate business. You are not only embracing technology, but you are showing that you are mastering it— you will use it as a tool, as it's meant to be used, but only let it change your business in positive ways. Be sure to make it easy for people to subscribe to your blog. The easier it is, the more folks will join, and the more will participate. Easy access is part of your viral marketing, too.

You can use blogs to demonstrate your expertise, rally the troops for a cause, help explain a trend or a solution to people, create a sense of community and a following, and establish your presence in the blogosphere—or, better yet, all of the above!

Tips for Setting Up, Designing, Hosting, and Writing/Recording Blogs or Podcasts

Our experience has taught us many tips for setting up, designing, hosting, and recording blogs and podcasts. Just as with the Web in its infancy, there really are no rules. However, certain tried and proven methods have become accepted, forming a sort of protocol. If you decide to venture outside these norms for the sake of innovation and "sexiness," you risk being perceived as an amateur. There's a fine line dividing innovation from silliness that you have to be careful not to cross.

Keep in mind that blogs and podcasts are tools, not solutions. If you have something meaningful to say, they can help you say it in an exciting and innovative way. However, if your words are not of much value to start with, the tools probably will not add value to them.

As you work on your blog and podcast, keep asking yourself the following question: Is my content useful and unique? If it's useful but not unique, then why should an individual visit your blog or podcast over another? If it's unique but not useful, you may get only an initial surge in traffic followed by a drop-off or a lot of one-time visitors. However, if it's both useful and unique, people will come and keep coming back.

As with all your marketing activities, keep the customer as the focus. Can you distinguish the subtle difference between the following two statements?

1. Provide the customer with what the customer wants.
2. Provide the customer with what you want the customer to know.

The first statement starts with the customer, while the second statement starts with you. The real estate industry has reached a stage where the average customer does not need to be taught the ABCs of buying and selling a home. Therefore, don't use your blogs and podcasts to present yourself as a sort of elementary school teacher. Rather, showcase yourself as a dynamic resource whom your customers can use to fill in knowledge gaps. Each customer is different, so make sure that your content is appropriate and interesting to a wide spectrum of audiences.

Setting up a blog or a podcast is like setting up any business. You need to start with a mission statement and answer the following question: What do I want to accomplish? The loftier your goals, the more critical the mission statement.

The first step in designing a blog is to determine whether you want it to be stand-alone or part of a platform. In other words, do you want to dedicate a personal website to your blog, or would you rather use a website company that provides blogging services (e.g., Blogger or WordPress.com)? Certainly the latter option is easier and less expensive, and such a site would probably be easier to locate using a search engine. However, you would sacrifice uniqueness both with the site's domain name and its look and feel.

Finally, when it comes to writing and recording blogs and podcasts, it's best to start with a specific and measurable plan. This means having several time-based milestones to meet specific and measurable tasks. For example, tasks that you could work towards completing in one month are "I will have ten unique entries in my blog" or "I will have recorded the introduction and conclusion to my reoccuring podcast."

Dynamic Web Sites and Changing Your Business Model

Last in our introduction to Web v2 technologies are dynamic websites. The term *dynamic* is basically the opposite of *static,* which means stationary or unchanging. Therefore, dynamic websites are those that change constantly in response to user commands. All aspects of these websites, such as text and images, can change on the fly. This technology began in the early 1990s with the advent of Common Gateway Interface (CGI) scripting. Languages like JavaScript, Perl, and ASP.NET can be used to program dynamic websites.

Domain Names—So Many Choices!

The domain name that you choose is absolutely critical. Much like naming a business, it must reflect something meaningful. Keep it short and catchy—think of Google and Yahoo! and Microsoft. A long, difficult business name or website address will keep you hidden. Being succinct and distinct is key. Keep it memorable (you want them coming back) and keep it simple and relevant. Companies like Google that make a brand name out of an unfamiliar word are a rarity in marketing. eBay and Hotmail are two more examples of sites whose names didn't necessarily reflect the business model yet became famous. Most don't work this way. Take for instance the Bank of America. We don't go to *www.bankingrocks.com* to get to BofA! We go to *www.bofa.com.*

You can probably think of countless other sites for which this holds true, particularly in finance and real estate. These companies already had brands, and their names were an important part of their brand equity. Chances are you do, too. It may simply be your name. For example, Dani's site at *www.drdaniellebabb.com* uses her name, which her students and clients already knew. And it doesn't need to be complicated to work, either.

We can already tell you that finding a domain name, especially one with words that are relevant to the real estate industry, will be an arduous process. Consider using *.biz* as an alternative to *.com* (pronounced "dot com"). Because it's used less frequently than *.com,* a *biz* address will expand the number of choices. When you use a site to find a domain, usually it will tell you what similar matches are available. We strongly suggest that you invest time and effort in this task, because you're going to be stuck with whatever you choose and your business will be identified with that domain name. Remember, just as in the nonvirtual world, there are trademarks that should not be violated. Don't take chances by choosing a name that someone else may claim as his/her own!

Even if you're not ready to build a site, you should still come up with a domain name now and register it. It's very inexpensive to do so. A company like NameSecure at *www.namesecure.com* can help you get started and even make suggestions if your preferred domain name has been taken. You may regret not reserving the name later on if someone else registers it. You can go to *www.networksolutions. com* and input some domain names to see if they're available. It is a lot of fun, actually—give it a shot!

A domain name is more then just something you type into a Web browser. It's a reflection of your business. If you think of something creative, something catchy, or something you think you might want to use in the future, have a company like NameSecure or countless other organizations to hold a domain name for you for a nominal charge (under $50/year). If you use NameSecure (which we have used for years to host our sites), you can create mailboxes and even forward mail to any address that you like. NameSecure will host your entire site with email and domain name for a few bucks a month. If you think that you'd like to create other sites to use in the future, you can use NameSecure to buy the domain name and just hold onto it until you are ready to build the site.

After you have a name, you can begin to build your dynamic website. A dynamic website is essentially a Web page with an interactive element that responds to inquiries or to various selections. It may change based on content or conditions of the user as well. Let's say the user has an account on the website that you have created and selects different features of interest. As these features become available, the website generates emails automatically to alert the user, update the page when they log in, and show alerts; better yet, the site may update them based on information they provide in a profile without user intervention. The site may also reload Web pages after a particular selection is made or something is known about the user. For example, Amazon's site could be considered dynamic; it uses previous knowledge about your last visit to display items that may be of interest. Sometimes sites react to a posted form, something in the URL that is specific to the user, browser rules, or time and calendar information (stored and logged in a database server).

If you go to a site whose drop-down menus and screen change based on what your mouse is hovering over, that is interactive. If you go to a site that remembers your preferences, that is interactive. Think of ways that you can offer creative items for your visitors, but also think about what information is relevant about them and how it will influence the data you'll display on the page. You can even allow your visitors to select the color scheme of your site and truly personalize it for themselves! Some sites do this with "cookies" (small files placed on users' computers by a Web server for tracking purposes), but some use other programming techniques.

If you want to include these types of options, you'll discuss the technical options with a Web designer.

What's the Difference Between Web Version 1 and Web Version 2?

We agree with those who refer to dynamic websites as a key element of Web 2.0. But how are these sites different than regular Web pages? The Web 2.0 pioneers at O'Reilly Media have a great list of the differences on their website:

Web Version 1	Web Version 2
DoubleClick	Google AdSense
Ofodo	Flickr
Akamai	BitTorrent
Mp3.com	Napster
Brittanica Online	Wikipedia
Personal Websites	Blogging
Evite	Upcoming.org and EVDB
Domain Name Speculation	Search Engine Optimization
Page Views	Cost Per Click
Screen Scraping	Web Services
Publishing	Participation
Content Management Systems	Wikis
Directories (taxonomy)	Tagging ("folksonomy")
Stickiness	Syndication

If you're familiar with some of these sites and features, you can see how Web 2.0 uses self-reliance and self-service. It also relies heavily on algorithms; that is, the computer makes the decision for the user based on information that it collects. Web 2.0 also attempts to harness collective intelligence. Hyperlinking based on user content, page ranks, and collective activity from all users (think Amazon.com and eBay) makes these systems very powerful.

Web 2.0 is the ultimate "open source" software, and we see this in Wikipedia or Flickr with their collaborative organizational methods. Blogging is an intimate element of Web 2.0, as are RSS feeds (a format used to publish digital content). Permalinks (used in blogs to maintain a permanent link to a past entry) also contributed to the success of Web 2.0 and the blogosphere, which is the peer-to-peer equivalent of Usenet (a global Internet discussion system) and bulletin boards.

In this new Web 2.0 model, it is unclear who "owns data," and ownership has yet to be decided as organizations collect intelligence and data and publicly display it for others to download, view, or use as they wish. In this new model, users are codevelopers, helping to develop the site or the blog and dramatically contributing to its content and success. This environment requires bloggers to treat their customers or their visitors in an entirely new way.

Ultimately, Web 2.0 is a fuller realization of Web 1.0 that uses the technology to its next greatest potential. It is user-rich in content; it binds all user experiences together. Web 2.0 requires services, not just plain old packaged software. It requires control over unique, hard to re-create data sources that get richer as more people use them. It harnesses collective intelligence and trusts users as developers. It leverages the "long tail" through customer service and provides software above the level of a single device. It uses lightweight interfaces; development models; and, perhaps even more importantly, business models.

Think of ways you can create a site that is unique to your visitors and relevant to the real estate industry. Why are they coming to your site? You need to do marketing analysis to find out—then be sure to give them exactly what they want!

Web 2.0 Inconsistency

If you ask ten people about Web 2.0, you will be given ten relatively similar yet inconsistent messages. In this book, we'll clarify the most important element—what Web 2.0 *means* to you and how you can apply it. There will no doubt be more versions in the future. In fact, there has been murmur on some blogs regarding Web 3.0. According to some initial perspectives, Web 3.0 seeks to "mine meaning" rather than just present data. Right now, Web 2.0 is the space in which real estate professionals need to play. However, here's how real estate business might roll out in the near future.

Currently, a prospective homebuyer may perform a home search based on specific criteria, like zip code, square footage, and number of bedrooms. The results that a website returns are accurate based on the cognitive desires of the searcher. But what if the Web could provide its own recommendations based on the lifestyle of the searcher? For example, a couple looking to purchase a home may indicate the following:

> We've got two kids aged 5 and 3, with a third on the way. We also have a dog. We love having our family over for barbeques. We usually don't have much time to cook meals from scratch, so we always maintain an inventory of heat-and-serve and ready-to-eat items. At the end of a long day, we love snuggling up as a family in front of the TV. By the way, mom stays at home with the kids, so we're on a single income.

Based on this input, Web 3.0 would present the family with new options, much as a traditional real estate agent would do after meeting the family and determining what type of home would make them happy. For instance, one option might be an affordable four-bedroom home with a large yard, standard kitchen, and big family room that is close to a good elementary school. Web 3.0 would basically render the standard input-output search engines obsolete and instead behave like a human agent. At this point, you should be thinking, "Where am I going to create a niche for myself when this technology arrives?"

Indeed, Web 3.0, and even Web 2.0, will make new demands of you. This is where the creative element comes in. You must create interesting forums where people who have common interests can share-and-tell. You must create the ability for them to comment on content that you present and learn more about you. You must create a website that reflects your personality and what is important and relevant to you. That common interest may be only your blog, or it may be an entire virtual community that you have set up around your practice. It may be a photo album you have set up of the insides of houses you've sold, or it may be tips on your particular community for other real estate professionals. It might be a forum where out-of-towners can learn about your locale before moving, or it might be a set of tools that your clients can use to value your work. With the right Web designer or Web architect, your imagination is the only limit.

2 Maximize Commissions

SALES PROFESSIONALS IN every industry want to maximize commissions. Real estate is no different—commissions are a staple of the real estate professional's income. That is, after all, the reason for doing business: to make a living. Our goal as technologists is to show you how you can use podcasts, blogs, and Web 2.0 to make more money. You can use technology to flourish in this rapidly changing marketplace.

The two primary ways to maximize commissions are to 1) minimize costs and 2) increase profits by selling more expensive homes, selling more homes, or charging more. Sellers don't want to pay full commissions, so the pressure is on to deliver the best possible service. You need every available tool to maximize your earnings! So how can you maximize commissions using podcasts? Let's take a look.

Using Podcasts to Maximize Commissions

The great thing about podcasts and other features of New Media is that they can temporarily take your place. These tools are so rich and vibrant that they can actually be substitutes for you, giving you the time and flexibility to do other things. They allow you to create and maintain a community and only log in as demand for your content requires. Imagine creating a podcast and using it over and over for all your showings. Instead of driving your clients around or meeting them at properties, you can simply direct them to a Web address that they can access in the comfort and privacy of their own homes. We're not implying that you can do your whole job remotely, but if you do technology right, you sure can come close!

What should you podcast? Lots of things! Your office, for instance—why not showcase your team along with a short podcast that contains interviews and advice? Rather than a clickable "meet the team" link that shows names and titles, you can include audio interviews, videos, and more. Podcasts allow you to show your desire to educate clients—and showcase your expertise—about a particular issue they may face. You can also podcast your suggestions for negotiating a deal. That way, while educating clients, you are also documenting their need for you. In the marketplace, clients hear mixed messages about their need for a real estate professional, so here is your chance to reinforce your message subtly. Include your advice to those who are listing a home on how to attract buyers' agents and what co-op commission to offer. Explain how to find a mortgage, with mentions of or links to your favorite business partners, of course. Explain what *escrow* means and how it works. A podcast can be a weekly or monthly ten-minute recorded message, linked from your blog, of course, and perhaps even fed using RSS. Or it can be a video newsletter that everyone who has subscribed to your site receives regularly (with opt-out options, of course!).

Is It Important to Maintain High-Quality Podcasts and Blogs?

"High quality" is certainly a subjective term. To us, a high-quality podcast or blog is one that leads to exponential growth for you in terms of increased visits; emails; phone calls; and, most importantly, listings. Therefore, the quality of podcasts and blogs should be measured in the value they add to your business. Even if we sat down with you and put our heads together to come up with a blog or a podcast that contained valuable information, appeared interesting, and looked good, it might not be successful. Ultimately, you might have to use a format that includes superficial information and a more sedate visual style. The important thing is that it works for your business.

It's very difficult to come up with a podcast or a blog that achieves success immediately, no matter how "high quality" it appears to be. Trial and error determines exactly what constitutes "high quality" to your particular subset of customers. Consider the prior successes that you've had with existing marketing materials and start there. Keep in mind that you are probably the ideal person to determine the contents of your blog and website. After a while, you'll know exactly what type of information to include and how to present it. Then you'll know for sure that your podcast or blog is of the highest quality!

How Many Podcasts and Blogs Should I Create?

How is it possible to target a niche while at the same time diversifying your clientele? The answer is to have multiple podcasts and blogs. The dilemma with being too focused is that you may spark a great deal of interest but only from a few individuals. The dilemma with being too diversified is that you'll attract a broad spectrum of people but probably only at a superficial level.

Therefore, why not have something specific to offer everyone? For example, you can create one main blog with a few additional blogs with specific focuses (e.g., selling, buying, investing). You can do the same with podcasts.

Getting Your Message Out There—But Where Is "There"?

There is not as unspecific as it seems. *There* is your community, your potential clients, your user base, your locale, your business partners, and your colleagues. We all know that real estate is local— local people, including those moving to your area, are your *there*. Getting your message out is one of the most confusing stages of the process, so we are going to dedicate a bit of space here to explain exactly how it's done.

One of the ways that we get messages out is by using a technology called RSS. RSS stands for "Really Simple Syndication" in the Web 2.0 world, or "Rich Site Summary" in the Web 1.0 world. This sounds really technical, and it is on the back end, but how you and your customers use it isn't all that complicated. Essentially, feed readers or aggregators check a list of feeds on a user's behalf and simply display the updated information. It isn't tough to send content, either. Two popular feeders and readers are YourLiveWire (*www.yourlivewire.net*) and NewsGator (*www.newsgator.com*). Do you have a new podcast? Tell people about it using an RSS feed. Also, tell people about it by posting in your blog, managing your subscriptions, and frequently updating your website with the latest and greatest collection of podcasts you have to offer.

Say you want to maximize a commission on a particular home, either by selling the home for a greater amount or increasing the seller's commission rate. You can do both using podcasts! Perhaps the seller gives a testimonial about the home, including features and upgrades, in a podcast, which is then hyperlinked from the MLS entry or from your website. Another option is to provide tiered commission structures in which those paying the highest commissions get to take advantage of your technological savvy and attract more buyers to their listings. Podcasts can replace virtual tours. Why have a 360-degree graphic with no commentator when you can have the seller or the agent showing the new miniblinds and the hardwood floors, taking a "walk upstairs," feeling the iron handrail, and opening the doors to the master suite? Think creatively—and try to use this technology in your listings. Instead of wasting an entire Saturday driving your clients around to view ten different homes, why not just show them the two homes that they've targeted after viewing all the podcasts?

Dos and Don'ts of Podcasting

As with anything, there are some rules. Some are social norms that we may not be aware of, like avoiding capital letters in emails (capital letters indicate that you are screaming, which is rude). An Internet search will turn up plenty of netiquette sites. There are some dos and don'ts to podcasts and blogs as well. An article on Podblaze (*http://blog.podblaze.com*) discusses the importance of understanding podcast best practices. We'll explain a few of the most relevant to real estate professionals.

It is important to remember that podcasts are an extension and reflection of yourself. A "good" podcast that shows your clients what you can do for them can have profoundly positive effects on your business, while a poorly produced podcast can actually be detrimental. It's better not to podcast than to do it badly. Your clients will compare your podcasts with those of your competitors. If yours appear amateurish in comparison, unfortunately so will you. No one expects you to be a full-time blogger or podcaster with the absolute best technology, but you should invest a little. Just as a cheesy-looking business card wouldn't be overlooked, neither will a podcast full of errors and poor-quality video and sound. Lots of sites (and other bloggers) offer tips on how to be successful at blogging and podcasting. The latest information is constantly changing, so it's good to visit these sites regularly and look for updates.

Some of the best practices are similar to those of any marketing campaign but with a unique twist—return visits. Most marketing is a one-shot campaign where you get business for a period of time. The benefit of online marketing is that you can create a buzz about yourself and your work that, if done correctly, is viral. You need to know your target market, just as you would with any marketing campaign. You need to make sure your site and your podcasts are clear and organized, making it easy to locate relevant content. You need to make sure that your podcasts stay on topic and don't veer off, becoming irrelevant to your audience, who will tune out. Having a script isn't a bad idea, but on the other hand, you don't want to seem so scripted that you sound like a commercial. Be sure that you edit the podcast both for quality and for content—both critical if you want users to take you seriously and recommend the podcast to others. Try to keep your information new and newsworthy. Try to engage people, and try to think of a new spin on an old topic or a new topic altogether.

When you really think about it, this isn't much different than any other type of marketing. You wouldn't send out a brochure or a flyer without editing it first, right? You wouldn't use a disorganized message or scattered notes, and you wouldn't just blindly send out your information without doing some research to make sure the return on investment is there. The same principles apply online.

If you want to add video *and* sound, consider using tools that make a high-quality product efficiently. Check out the blog at *http://coolmel.zaadz.com/blog* for lots of examples of successful people using blogs and podcasts and tips on how they do it. It's not related to real estate, but it should still give you some great ideas. Upload your video to appropriate locations, including potentially YouTube and even Revver (*http://one.revver.com/revver*). Be sure also to check out FreeVLog (*www.freevlog.org*) as well as Pro PR (*http://propr.ca*), a public relations site with lots of great tips and information on podcasting and video blogs.

Do your best to invest in good hardware; if you have a poor-quality video, people will associate you with poor quality. Even small-time bloggers and podcasters are using sophisticated—yet relatively inexpensive—tools. Make sure your environment is free from distracting noise, too, and test out your microphone. Be sure you listen to your own podcast before you publish. (We know that for many of you, hearing your own voice is agonizing, but you have to do it!) Also, be sure—we cannot emphasize this enough—to check the end user license agreement (EULA) with the service that you use to distribute your information. You may find out that you don't own your own content, which is not a good thing! Most sites don't co-opt users' content this way, but you don't want to get stuck with one that does.

Be sure that you are featured in your own podcast. Your podcasts are about *you,* not about people that you can hire for a podcast. You don't want your business to look so staged that it doesn't accurately represent you or your work. Dani had a client who used to stage photos, and while this practice isn't uncommon, she wondered where the professional-looking people all went when she visited the office. The company wasn't capitalizing on the energy and youth in the office, instead making the staff dress 20 years older for the photo, and they weren't accurately representing their work. The employees were a bunch of former frat boys who were doing remarkable things, but their portraits in business suits made the company look like any other firm. Think of what makes you different. Represent the heck out of it. If you are proud of it, if it serves your clients well, and if it makes sense, it will appeal to a particular community of viewers and clients.

One goal when you are doing all of this, of course, is to create a sense of community and personality so that people get a sense of who you are and what you stand for. Professional actors won't do this for you. Sure, they can make your podcast more attractive, but using them distances yourself from your viewers, certainly not what you want. Also, you need to be brief when you deliver your cast. Keep any overt attempts at self-promotion brief and as subtle as possible. You might want someone else to review your content before you put it on the Web. Get their opinion—ask if your podcast is too promotional or if it offers enough good information to keep people coming back. Try imagining that you are telling a story or just having a casual conversation with a prospect (or a partner, depending on your target). Consider removing banner ads—even though they can be a great source of revenue, they can annoy your potential visitors. Make the content easy to get to; you don't want people wading through link after link to find material that they care about. We know that sites have greater click-through rates when they are less complicated.

You may already know that many advertisers are turning to product placement instead of traditional ads. You can access our own blog on Realtown Blogs and look up Real Estate 2.0 or the authors' names. We also have our work and links to our blogs at *www.drdaniellebabb.com*. Consider this option to advertise your blog or podcast, placing yourself in the right areas of the Internet to draw attention to your work.

Be creative, but be creative in different ways. What seems interesting and eye-catching the first time may quickly become old and stale if reused too often. Several quick and witty spots will go much farther than one long, drawn-out one.

Remember, you're not standing on top of a soapbox preaching. Rather, you're trying to reach an audience that is sophisticated and understands technology to educate them on the topic you know best. Therefore, be careful not to patronize them! The importance of not underestimating your audience cannot be understated. With technology, and in particular the Internet, consumers are more educated and they expect more. How many times have you called tech support only to be asked if your computer is plugged in? How infuriated were you with the question? If you dumb down your material, you may be perceived as offensive or patronizing. Assume a certain level of understanding, then use the medium to elaborate and provide more information as you see fit.

It is best to place your ads throughout your podcast, not just at the beginning and the end. In fact, it's probably best to not have an ad at the beginning at all. Viewers will lose their excitement if the first thing they see or hear is an ad. In fact, they may start to perceive the entire production as a sort of infomercial—certainly not the impression you want to give. You want users to watch the whole podcast, not to fast-forward through the beginning as we all used to do on our VCRs during the preview section before a movie.

Don't you hate all the obnoxious sounds and yells that you hear on the radio? These are designed to grab your attention so you don't switch to another station. If a podcast is produced properly, you shouldn't have to resort to such desperate measures.

Here's a tip: Rather than using scripts, try practicing a few times unscripted. The casualness in your voice may actually make your podcast sound more informative and less like an infomercial. The authors have done many of these, and just as some presenters do better without slides because they sound more natural, the same is true for podcasts. Try it, and if you don't like the way you sound, move to a more scripted version.

A podcast viewer has already taken the necessary steps to prepare to experience your message. The hard part is already over, because you already have the viewer's attention. The individual is a qualified lead, because he/she wants to be on your site. Now your task becomes maintaining that attention and offering something useful.

Hosting Your Blog

Once you have used your camera to create your video blog or podcast, you'll need a hosting company or your own website to support it. Companies like Libsyn (Liberated Syndication) help you get your video or sound bites out there. If you Google Libsyn, you will find lots of sources to link you to the software. They don't charge for bandwidth, so you don't pay more if more people view your goods, and they let you manage an RSS feed yourself. Their solutions range from \$5 to \$30. Be sure to watch your statistics so you know who is viewing your podcasts and how many people have subscribed.

Okay, I Need Podcasting. Now What?

So you want to create a podcast, but you have no equipment. Believe it or not, there are tools out there that will let you call a telephone number, record your speech, and create a podcast! You can even put them on your own website in addition to using them at the hosting site. One of the initial founding companies of such technology was ODEO (*http://odeo.com*). Today, there's also gabcast (*http://gabcast.com*), hipcast (*www.hipcast.com*), and Gcast (*www.gcast.com*). Among these, our favorite is hipcast. Hipcast allows you to post to blogs, create video, create podcasts, create audio via telephone or upload, and record your podcast or audio online, and it is super easy to use. For more information, check out the recommendations at *http://odeo.com* and *http://podcasting-tools.com*.

If you are part of a real estate office, you may want to partner up with one or more other agents. This strategy would save you money and increase exposure for the entire office. In fact, you can create a podcast for your office and take turns with other agents in presenting featured topics, homes, etc. At this point, you should be starting to view podcasts like any other advertising medium that you already use.

One of the things people ask us regularly is whether iPods are needed for podcasts. The answer is no—you do not need an iPod to access a podcast. The similarity of the terms may be confusing. There are other many ways to listen to podcasts, including on the Internet through software. To make your podcasts available to your clients, you'll need to do a few things, none of them very time consuming. First, you need to record an audio file, and then you need to put that file into an RSS 2.0 feed. Sounds complicated? It isn't. Many tools are available to help you. If you Google "create a podcast," you will find a lot of free software. One site we like a lot is Download.com (*www.download.com*), as it has a lot of free tools (and not only for podcasting). We also list lots of resources at the end of this book in Appendix B.

Just like with anything else, you get what you pay for. You need to have audio recording equipment, and you can use anything from a $10 computer microphone to studio-quality sound equipment. If you are doing virtual tours or open houses, you will want strong audio, but try not to pick up ambient noise that may scare off potential buyers. We suggest experimenting to find the right balance for your budget and requirements. The better you want your quality to be, the more expensive your equipment must be.

Equipment is only an initial expense. If you decide to host your own podcasts, bandwidth will be a reoccurring cost. Buying extra bandwidth, however, should be a welcomed expense, as it will indicate that a lot of people are downloading your podcasts! If you want to host your own podcast, you'll need to submit it to a directory. This is how you generate interest and let people know about your information and what you provide to your real estate community. Not using a directory is like having a great business with no advertising—you wouldn't do that and expect results. We hear a lot of people grumble over low podcast hits, but this poor performance is probably due to their lack of advertising. You have to make sure your site comes up in search engines, so be sure you promote it and that you use a host site that lets you enter key words so search engines can find you.

Remember that there are no real size limits to podcasts, unless you are using a hosting company that limits size (most do not). Of course, the higher the quality of your podcast, the larger the file size, and the larger the file size, the more chance that you will discourage viewers with slower connections. Larger files can alienate those with dial-up or other low-bandwidth connections. Nonetheless, file size is directly correlated with quality, and you don't want to skimp on quality because of size. To keep quality high but file size within reason, keep the length of the podcast in your mind at all times and have a plan for where you want it to go.

If you decide to integrate music, be careful of royalty fees unless you are using royalty-free music (which exists—just Google it!). You can either try to obtain licenses from record companies or use music that is not subject to copyright protection, generally American recordings made before February 15, 1972. (Remember, a reissue of a pre-1972 recording is considered new and, thus, protected.) Of course, plenty of music is out there, much of which you can purchase for use. Find out what the creator or owner allows you to use it for, and for how long. Whatever you do, don't take permissions lightly.

Check out these sites that are related to using music in podcasts:

- *Bestkungfu Weblog* (*http://www.bestkungfu.com/archive/date/2005/02/podcasting-music-and-the-law*). This great site takes you through the licensing steps in detail.

- *Podcasting News: "Podcast-Legal Music"* (*http://www.podcastingnews.com/topics/Podcast-Legal_Music.html*). This is another great site with many links to other websites that contain music that you can use legally.

- *Creative Commons: "Podcasting Legal Guide"* (*http://wiki.creativecommons.org/Podcasting_Legal_Guide*). Look halfway down the page to read about five instances where you don't need permission to use music.

Blogging Your Way to Greater Commissions

Blogs will also help you maximize your commission. If you have an active blog (a blog becomes active through promotion, viral marketing, word of mouth, time, and persistence), then you will have a following of people who undoubtedly look to you first when listing, particularly if they know you are savvy with technology. Think of blogs as high-tech replacements for the personalized refrigerator magnets, calendars, and notepads that you've always given out to make sure your name remains in the line of sight of prospective clients.

Blogs can be a great feedback loop for you to learn what your competitors are charging for what services. Blogs can help your clients stay connected with each other and, more importantly, with *you*. Blogs will encourage discussion and keep you in the forefront of viewers' minds. Remember that bloggers essentially become a part of your business, and so you need to provide them the tools to do that. Use blogs that allow individuals to be notified when messages are posted and allow people to use tools to create links, look back on threads, and comment. Why not have a blog for an area or neighborhood you sell in? Perhaps even experiment with a blog for a particular house you are selling? This strategy could be particularly helpful with a high-end home or one that is in excellent condition and probably not appealing to a fixer-upper. Come to think of it, why not have a blog that people can use to learn the tricks of fixing up a dilapidated home?

Some world-renowned geeks we admire at Zillow.com have come up with a great five-part tutorial on blogs. They call it "Roadmap for New Bloggers." These people know what they're talking about; within one year after its launch, the company made the cover of *Fortune* magazine! Technologists love what some would call "rogue" companies like Zillow.com. It provides awesome service and a new model or paradigm to an existing business, and it is a trendsetter. You should pay attention to Zillow.com; it is a company to watch. Here's a recap of some of its advice for bloggers:

> What will it take to make your blog successful? How can you create traffic and be perceived as an expert in your field? After all, isn't that what it's all about? You need to keep in mind that all these things are achievable, but they take time. You're going to find that regular customers are like gold. Sure, you'll get clients who wander in every now and then, but those are not going to be the keys to your

success. Therefore, it becomes vital to transform a first-time customer into a regular one. By this point, you should be thinking about branding. After all, your blog is part of your marketing effort. Keep this in mind as we go through the next set of suggestions.

Content needs to be relevant, fresh, and timely. Attracting and maintaining visitors go hand in hand; you need one to get the other. Once you get proper placement in search engines, you need to keep it by giving people reasons to come back again and again.

Are you lost with what you should write about? Focus on what you know. After all, this is why your visitors are seeking people like you. In the Zillow Blog, anything and everything related to the real estate industry is discussed. Of course, your blog will not be the only one of its kind; therefore, the specific topics discussed in your blog should be at least somewhat unique. Put yourself in the place of your audience and ask yourself if your blog is boring, captivating, or somewhere in between. Have your friends and family join and participate. Ask them for their honest feedback.

We get asked all the time, "I have nothing to write about—what do I say?" Many people have famous blogs based upon their journals! You could talk about all sorts of things, but you should write about things that are unique, even if only to your local market (all real estate is local, right?). Try to get a sense for what everyone else is talking about and go in a different direction. We've seen lots of successful bloggers talk about everything from open house tips or horror stories to the general real estate market in their area (which, by the way, we think is a highly overused blog topic). If you're still having trouble thinking of ideas, sit and ask yourself this question: When people talk with me, what do I tell them that they are most fascinated by? Is it your incredible wealth of information about the layout of 1980s homes? How property taxes affect sales? That the real estate market isn't really in a bubble and you have proof? The key is passion. If you are passionate, it will come across in your work. Who wants to visit a blog that just talks about the same boring statistics? There are many famous blogs that you're competing with that already do just that; find a new niche.

Make sure that you are the focus of your blogs. Have a strong voice. Get to know your bloggers and help them to get to know you. Make them feel like they know you on a personal level. Of course, if you don't appear interesting, then they're not going to be too eager to get to know you. Use WordPress.com and Blogger for practice. Start out with a private blog (just you and some close friends and family), then make it public once you gain confidence in your blogging abilities.

Writing can be tough. No one ever masters it. You have to decide what kind of tone you want your blog to take. Informal? Formal? If you want it to be formal and more on the serious side of things, you cannot write sloppily. If you want it to be informal and allow people to feel free to share opinions rather than just facts, you should do the same. The tone you set will carry throughout your work. One thing that helps us to get started is brainstorming. This may be especially useful for your first post! Take out a blank sheet of paper and write words all over the page; what comes to mind? What dots did you connect? These may be things to help you begin. If you want to spruce up your writing, go to the old thesaurus. Just be sure you are mostly free from grammatical mistakes. Everyone makes one here and there, but making too many mistakes may discredit you to some readers.

A blog platform refers to the look and feel of your blog. You need first to decide whether you want to start off with a personal or a business blog. In either case, there are many sites out there that can help. On the personal side,

WordPress.com and Blogger are common platforms (and they're free!). On the business side, you can also use WordPress.com (not the free version, though), but also try TypePad and Movable Type. For real estate agents, ActiveRain, RSS Pieces, Tomato Blogs, and Blogging Systems are relevant. We also recommend that you check out the Zillow wiki pages. These pages are chock-full of information to help you shape your goals and about how various components play a role in your blog.

When it comes to hosting a blog on the Web, you can do one of two things: simply pay for a hosted blogging solution or install a blogging platform on your own hosted server (like GoDaddy.com and Dreamhost, for example). If you choose the first option, you'll find the setup process easy, because much of the work will be done by your service provider. Even if you choose the second option, you won't have much difficulty, as it is normally done with a "one-click install." Remember that you need not fret over the technological side. Focus on content and advertising, and your blog will be a success! We recommend paying a provider that allows you to enter search criteria and has components to let your Web developer integrate your blog into your own site. You may wish to get a recommendation from your Web developer or architect.

Customization of your blog is very important. To do this, you need to edit the "template" that you're using. There are many free templates out there that can be acquired from the websites mentioned above. Modifying the templates is a bit tricky. Usually, you're going to want to modify the "sidebar" portion. This is the part of the page that displays the information that you want all your users to see regardless of which individual blog post they happen to be reading. A sidebar should provide your readers with a good high-level introduction to yourself and the content. It can include links, contact information, and a subscription link. Check out the following blog that focuses on creating blogs: *www.emilyrobbins.com/how-to-blog/*.

A useful tool you can have within your sidebar is a "Search" box. This is a quick way for viewers to search the contents of a particular blog they may be interested in. Every good blog should have one!

One part of Zillow's "Roadmap for New Bloggers" focuses on avoiding legal pitfalls. Remember that when you blog, you can be held liable much like a newspaper or television station. Blogs are actually much riskier, because the speed at which they can be updated makes it very difficult to keep track of what's happening. Always err on the side of caution and avoid such things as hearsay that you feel may be used against you if push came to shove. A blogger can certainly be accused of libel if he or she publishes false statements about someone, and can also be subject to legal damages. Though you are not liable if a someone posts libelous statements in your blog's comments section, if you republish them, you may be held to account. We are not attorneys, so please check with an attorney regarding these matters. The best thing to do is to publish only the truth. The "golden rule" certainly has a place here.

If you're going to use a lot of material from other sources, be sure to cite it. You are not allowed to post copyrighted material in your blog without first obtaining permission from the copyright holder, and it is important that you always give credit to the original source. Beyond that, if you intend to reuse a lot of material, you may want to get permission or talk with your attorney. In the past, only members of the media had to deal with these issues, and they were trained to do so. Bloggers are everyday people who aren't trained journalists and don't necessarily know what they are doing when it comes to intellectual property.

The First Amendment and the fair use doctrine do not give anyone free reign in posting. Section 107 of the

Copyright Act mentions four factors that should be considered when determining fair use:

1. The purpose and character of the use, including whether such use is of a commercial nature or is for nonprofit educational purposes
2. The nature of the copyrighted work
3. The amount and substantiality of the portion used in relation to the copyrighted work as a whole
4. The effect of the use upon the potential market for or value of the copyrighted work

Because you are ultimately trying to benefit financially from your blog, you need to be especially careful. When in doubt, obtain permission. Most of the time, none of these issues comes into play. However, there have been cases where problems have risen to the surface. Be sure you talk with your attorney if you hear any grumblings that you think may be an issue and follow the law. Zillow.com and other websites (do a search in Google for *libel blogs*) provide a lot of good information to keep you out of trouble and free to speak your mind.

Inbound links to your blog are probably the most effective method of achieving high rankings in search engines. In fact, both inbound and outbound links can be beneficial. Use links all over your blog. It's OK to link to other blogs because linking often results in return links back to yours.

To help search engines discover your blog, you can do some of the following—the more, the better:

- Make it easy to subscribe to your blog by using feed buttons and make sure that the content is relevant to real estate—and makes you *the* expert in the area you're promoting.

- Use only one URL. Don't have multiple addresses—for instance, don't have one site address for your company, one for your blog, and yet another for you! Try to integrate as much as you can.

- When writing your URL on any page, separate out the key words using hyphens if you need to do so, but don't use an underscore (_).

- Don't use the generic "title tag" that the blog provider gives you. Change it to reflect your specific blog, because this will be important for searching and for making the blog friendlier to users.

- Check with your blog host to see if it has search engine optimization (SEO) plug-ins, and if it does, use them.

- Use categories in your blog and make sure to include key words when picking these categories. If you are going to focus on the Seattle residential real estate market, use a very specific category.

- Use "sticky content" in each category page. This is basically a sentence that contains two or three key words that describe the category and remains at the top of the page. This reminds people why they are there, what you are the expert in, and how and why to stay on topic!

Once you've got some great content and have made it user-friendly, you've got to spread the word. Most readers of your blog will have gotten to it through an RSS feed. Here's how you can make it easier for them to read it:

- Subscribe to your blog in Technorati (*http://technorati.com*) and the other blog subscription services that you can find via your favorite search engine.

Don't forget real-estate-specific sites, too, and ask others to link to you!

- Make sure that each category in your blog is subscribable and then subscribe to all the categories. You want to know what others are saying. You won't necessarily automatically be kept abreast of the writing in your own blog, so subscribe to your own blog, too.

- Allow others to subscribe to each category, thus eliminating junk email that they get, giving them a sense of control and using Web 2.0 dynamic preferences.

- Make sure to post full text and not just summaries. People want the opportunity to read all the text.

- Include a site description, just as you would for any website.

The setup of the blog really is one of the easiest parts if you use the right tools. Focus your time and effort on creating a great-looking site, on providing lots of useful links and tips, and most importantly on developing your content and message—not just the actual words, but the implied message you are sending to visitors. What do the colors say? Are they soothing or powerful? Does it matter? Sure it does! Someone who wants a real estate professional to play hardball and negotiate with them on a pricey real estate deal may not want a website full of flowers and butterflies. On the other hand, a parent who works at or from home may find this appealing (or not—that is for you to decide). Know your client! You may want to ask a few test subjects what appeals to them. Have them look at a page blank of text, containing only the layout and design, and ask what message they got from the site. Be sure it reflects your personality; the more real it is, the more attractive it (and you) will be.

So how do you entice a conversation in your blog? First of all, make sure that you allow users to leave comments.

Comments are really what separates a blog from a regular website. Allow users to become an integral part of your website. This is free content that comes with no effort from you! In addition, it provides you with a method for measuring the appeal of your topics. A topic that receives many comments, even negative ones, is one that's of great interest. Comments are the equivalent of "letters to the editor."

Always listen to your readers. This is free advice that would otherwise cost you a lot of money. Don't second-guess the feedback that you get unless you think there is a serious flaw in the way it was collected. Also, don't feel that you have to be perceived as having all the answers. Your site visitors are going to be more apt to post if they feel that they can educate the community. It's okay for you to ask questions like "What do you think?" Be open and honest with your bloggers. Respond quickly to keep interest alive and try to respond to every question if feasible. If someone points out a factual error that you make (hey, it happens), correct it quickly and publicly thank the person who corrected you—this is no time for defensiveness!

There will be times that it's better not to respond. There is no point in beating up or putting down readers. Never take offense at negative comments that are directed at you personally, even if the person meant for them to be taken that way! Take the higher road.

Remember, you are the moderator of your blogging platform. This means that you have the ability to "tidy things up." Always delete spam and, whenever possible, block spammers from commenting further. You can always force users to register and log in to your blog to comment. This will reduce spam but may deter legitimate participation, so it's probably better not to require registration.

Trolls can be worse than spammers. A troll is a blog commenter who criticizes endlessly and is impossible to please. They will use every opportunity to harm you. They certainly have the right to do so, but it's best to ignore them and encourage others to do the same. Most people are smart enough to spot a troll, and often your fellow bloggers will take the person on verbally without your having to do anything. This response will eventually make the troll go away.

The following services can be considered "silent comments." These are methods other than actual comments by which you will know that other readers have been to your site:

- TrackBack (*http://en.wikipedia.org/wiki/Trackback*)
- Digg (*http://digg.com*)
- Five-star rating system
- Subscriber count
- MyBlogLog avatar (*http://mybloglog.com*)

Always remember to comment on other blogs. Actually, as a new blogger, that should be the first thing you do; comment on other blogs before working on your own. When you leave a comment, you can link back to your own blog. It's a kind of "you scratch my back and I'll scratch yours" system.

Use Web v2 to Be the Expert

Perhaps most useful for increasing commissions is using Web v2 to showcase your expertise. Who knows the area you represent better than you? Use the Web to create an excellent resource for information and as a place for people to get information on current pricing. Keep your information updated—nothing is a bigger turnoff to visitors than outdated info. It is counterintuitive to the spirit of the Web as a dynamic source of information. If visitors, even after just one visit, perceive your site as being static, they probably won't come back. A real estate agent in one of the authors' areas sends out a quarterly sheet showing the tracts of homes and the prices they sold for, as well as the prices of those in escrow. This could all be put online with an interactive map and a community blog to help people share thoughts on how to improve their property values, how to increase the value of the neighborhood, and how to find new strategies to price homes. This leads to trusting your community to help you, and you will help them back by applying the knowledge you gain from your built-in network.

Content Is King!

When people go to your site to look at your information before possibly listing their home with you, they should get content—not instructions to "call for more information." They went to the website for content, and having to call you defeats the purpose. If you have a service priced right, don't be afraid to make it clear what you are offering and why it is of value. Some agents may even choose to break down their commission structure into multiple options. For instance, tell your clients that if they want a standard virtual tour, it is free. If they want their home podcasted, the commission is 0.5 percent higher. If they want a blog about their home and its features, that is also 0.5 percent more, but a standard yard sign is free. Think about how you can unbundle services and make more money while giving each buyer control over what is important. This flexibility alone will increase your ability to sell, and your creativity in using technology will no doubt lead to greater success and a reputation for being an online expert.

You need to change the antiquated mind-set that states that you must meet people face to face to sell their home or help them find a new one. Your podcasts, blogs, and website, if done correctly, will give people the personal touch they need, while you devote your time to more productive aspects of your business. You will become much more efficient with your time when you start dealing with clients who have already been exposed to you and your services through the Internet. Learn to work smart, not hard. This is what the top producers do. The old adage that personal accessibility translates into sales is not as true as it used to be.

Get Started Fast Using Tools

In the next section, we'll look at sites and tools that will get you up and running quickly. It is important to mention that you can make additional money by selling access to other real estate agents who cannot afford full websites, selling memberships to brokers, selling advertising space to mortgage brokers and banks/lenders, generating leads for advertisers and partners, and leasing out websites to mortgage brokers (Henry 2006).

Don't be intimidated. You've already taken the biggest step by buying this book and deciding to venture into the new age of online real estate. Once you understand the concepts, most everything from that point is cookie-cutter. Of course, your personal touch is key.

Interactivity Is Critical

Be sure to understand and review the opportunities provided with interactive forms (those that change based on user input). The key here is *interactive*. You'll find an example to help generate ideas at *http://phpforms.net/demo.html*. Remember that to be interactive, the audience must be able to participate; in fact, they must feel that they aren't an audience at all but a part of the community that you have created—with a purpose, of course.

3 Increase Listings

YOU ALREADY KNOW that to increase listings, you need to draw more people into your homes for sale and make more people aware of your business. There are lots of ways to do this online with New Media. The concept is the same as with any other marketing venture but does have a few new twists. Sure full-color flyers are great, but how can those compare to a 360-degree narrated view of a home? Both of the authors of this book recently purchased homes, and when we used aggregator MLS engines, we were frustrated to see one picture or, worse yet, no picture at all! Realizing that many of you don't want to pay for such photos (or your companies don't), we'll help you consider other tools to help showcase these properties.

Sellers want to know that you have their best interests in mind, and many want to pay only for services they choose. They also want you, the expert, to tell them what they need to do to sell their home and get them a fair price. It isn't a bad idea to explain your business and home-selling philosophy on your website. This may comfort many potential clients who are not at ease with the current market, and it will reinforce their perception of your expertise.

Here's an idea that you might want to try out after you have the technology up and running. Take a laptop with you to your open houses and showcase your other listings for people who walk in. That's much more effective than simply handing them a couple of pieces of paper. We aren't suggesting replacing your traditional methods but rather supplementing them; showcase your tech savvy and your understanding of what educated clients want.

Combating the Unfriendly Media

Real estate professionals are getting a poor reputation in some media outlets, where stories claim they are overcharging and under-serving. Anyone following the many forums and blogs on this topic knows that agents are getting hammered for charging too much and increasing their commissions (a percentage of sales price) depending on the price of the home. To some people, this practice looks as though agents are unjustifiably increasing commissions without increasing their workload. This may be true for some agents, but most are simply the victims of a price war driven by online competitors that let owners list their own houses for small fees and provide partial service for much lower commissions. You can fight back by using both people and technology elements in your work. Offer the ease of the Internet-only companies (like communicating by email or text messaging without interrupting clients with a ringing phone) combined with the face-to-face business that you already do so well. Why not let the seller be a part of the blog about their home for sale and give the podcast themselves (unless, of course, they want you to handle it)?

We're living in an age of the educated consumer thanks largely to the quick and easy access to information offered by technology and, in particular, the Web. You must embrace technology or risk being left behind. Don't be known as the agent who simply collects listings and relies on the other party's agent to make the sale. Be proactive and avoid the nightmare that all agents have . . . the expired listing! Almost any agent can sell a home if given enough time, but that's not what you should aim for. You want to be known as the agent who turns homes around, the one with an equal number of "For Sale" and "Sold" signs. The technology we discuss in this book will help you become that agent. The process and the goals are time tested; the tools, however, are innovative.

You will increase listings because you will be the number one user of technology to promote homes in your area. You will increase listings because you create a community blog, because people know about you, and because the local newspaper interviewed you about your useful and creative marketing techniques.

You will also increase listings because consumers feel there is transparency in your business. How many of your clients wonder if your other clients got a better deal? Do they question if they got your "lowest commission rate"? When you don't answer or avoid the question, sellers think you are hiding something. Your business data is private, but the Internet is making almost every element of business transparent. People are willing to pay for good service, but they must feel as though they are getting a good deal. Why not list this information on the Web? Why not use a podcast to tell every homeowner what you'll do for them if they allow you to list their home? Why not create a blog that lets others post what you've excelled at, what you didn't quite do so hot (take this as informative, constructive criticism and respond appropriately), and what is "going strong" for their areas? Involving the community is a surefire way to increase awareness of your brand and your business, perhaps more so than the magnets and notepads we're all used to.

Bad-Mouthed in Blogs—Now What?

Some of you are thinking, "What if people really bad-mouth me in my blogs? My blog gives that insatiable 1 or 2 percent another avenue to make me look bad—and it's costing me money for them to do it, even if I don't deserve it!" Sometimes bad comments are the result of a troll, other times from legitimately upset or unhappy clients. We can completely relate; as authors, we get trashed in blogs by people who disagree, don't like what we write, or just flat out had a bad day. You won't be able to remove all of the criticism that comes your way. That's okay. The old adage "no publicity is bad publicity" is true, *if* you take the time to counter it. When a client says you are "not on top of things," show the community bloggers that you are on top of things by responding to the comment within two hours. If someone is trying to smear you, that is a different matter, and you should remove their posts and consider our section on libel in Chapter 2. But if the comments are just typical disagreements, show your strengths. Showcase your capabilities and take the feedback head-on!

Specific Tools to Increase Listings

Let's talk about some specific tools you can use to increase listings. The authors consulted a professional Web architect, a profession more elite than a traditional Web developer. A Web architect takes into account your business and your industry, knows the latest and greatest Web technology, and can integrate it to create a brand. Cheryl Ann Henry, a Web architect with many clients, says it is easy for real estate pros to set up businesses online. For under $500 and less than one day with a turnkey (out-of-the-box) solution, anyone can get started. Examples she specifically cites are: e-Classifieds® (*http://e-classifieds.net*) and The Real Estate Script (*http:// therealestatescript.com*), which uses Google Maps (*http://maps. google.com*) and satellite images of properties. Agents who want to publish their own listings may choose software like AtlantDesigns (*http://atlantdesigns.com/scripts/listings2*), and more enterprising agents may want to show other agents' listings and charge them a fee. For these agents, Brokerexec (*http://brokerexec.com*) is a good solution. For those who want to rent vacation homes, check out PHP Vacation Rental (*http://demo.phpvacationrental.com*); for real estate classifieds, My Real Estate (*www.phpclassifieds.info/realty/ demo*); and rentals, Online-Rent.com (*http://online-rent.com/demo. html*). You don't need to spend a lot of time and money trying to create the platform for your site; many companies have already created it for you!

Flash Technology

If you really want to increase the potential for listings, consider adding flash maps. These are interactive geographic maps of a country, state, city, etc., that users can click on to obtain further information (e.g., to find "for sale" listings).

Note that while these sites are relatively inexpensive, and getting a site up and running isn't really expensive, either, it is best to get the value of an experienced Web professional if you really want to build something dynamic. Developers use more than templates, and you'll get something that looks far more professional. Lots of copycat websites are out there already. Yours needs to have a distinctive look.

What you want to pay attention to when viewing these sites isn't so much the interface, because all of that can easily be changed, but for features. Notice at phpMyRealty.com (*http://phpmyrealty.com*) that the listing alerts are a pull technique that push alerts to subscribers. The cost to set it up versus the potential to make money is tremendous. What makes these sites dynamic? The administration is on the back end, so the real estate professional can add, modify, or remove listings, create slide shows, etc. Changes can also be applied on the front end, so changes are reflected for the visitor in real time. The sites run themselves for the most part, because those who contribute to them run them. Everything is constantly changing, fresh looking, intriguing, and engaging for the viewer. This is an important retention element and will help you get more listings. These sites are low maintenance, and you don't need to be a tech whiz to run them (Henry 2006).

Web 2.0 Tools You Can Use to Increase Listings

Some view technological tools as competitive with their work and assume they will damage sales. Don't fall for this mind-set! Today's technology-savvy consumer expects you to embrace tools. Here are a few more to get you started.

Demographic Tools

Consider offering demographic information via links from your site. Consumers can visit the website of the county they are looking to move to or purchase property in. Usually companies or organizations publish demographic data and the job or economic outlook of the area. A consumer site that can't be overlooked, despite its age in the marketplace, is MapQuest (*www.mapquest.com*). This site provides an incredibly information-rich presentation and useful data your potential clients can use to make knowledgeable decisions. You can simply query a search engine like Google as well and type in key words, such as *demographics Austin,* to pull up demographic data on that particular market. Also, take some time to explore terraXsite™ (*http://terraxsite.com*), distributed by the *Real Estate Journal,* for additional information.

Another way to pull up demographic data is by zip code. Often, this approach provides more specific information than simply typing in a city name, because cities have both good and bad areas. Zip codes are more specific and tend to be drawn around economic boundaries (which came first, the zip code or the income?). Check out California State University—Northridge's "Community Information by Zip Code" at *http://library.csun.edu/mfinley/zipstats.html.*

Another great demographic source is MelissaData (*www.melissadata.com/lookups/*). This tool allows consumers to search over 30 databases. Try it out yourself and encourage your Web visitors to use it. You will be asked fewer questions about demographics if you do business with an educated consumer base.

Mortgage Calculators and Interest Rate Comparison Tools

We cannot for the life of us imagine why someone without a long-term relationship with an honest banker would consider purchasing an investment property or residence without looking into what banks in their area are offering for interest rates—or for that matter using aggregator sites like E-Loan (*http://eloan.com*). Individual banks only offer *their* interest rates on loans, not their competitors'. Mortgage brokers are often adding so much to the cost of a loan that the consumer would be far better off going directly to the lender. Thanks to some online educational sites, more people are realizing this. The Internet is certainly bridging the knowledge gap between seller/service provider and consumer. Rate comparison companies, like LendingTree (*http://lendingtree.com*), started their own niche: "Let banks compete for your business." Even LendingTree works only with some banks. LendingTree is a good place to start if a consumer is serious about receiving bids right away. E-Loan is also considered reputable by consumers. You may wish to link to these sites or, better yet, integrate your data with up-to-the-second information from these sites. You can visit their pages on partnering to figure out how—or turn the task over to your Web architect. There you have it—instant credibility!

Take a look at Yahoo! Finance's section on Homes at *http://finance.yahoo.com*, which is loaded with relevant information for you. If your clients want to know the current mortgage rates, they can check out Bankrate.com (*http://bankrate.com*), which provides a world of information on this subject. It will also provide you with a tool to calculate how much home a person can afford and give you information on who has the cheapest loans in an area. Consumers can also use their favorite search engine for other providers of such handy (and cost-saving) information. The Mortgage Professor provides a variety of spreadsheets for consumers to compare various mortgages and offers at *http://mtgprofessor.com/spreadsheets.htm*. When you visit this site, you will be amazed at the number of spreadsheets that site creator Jack Guttentag has had on the Internet for years!

Why not offer these tools to your clients directly from your website? Your website can become a sort of portal for the industry. Often, not only will they save you time, but your clients will appreciate your offering services to them (much more than they would a refrigerator magnet!). No need to reinvent the wheel here; lots of great companies are already doing this stuff. The Web is referral based; companies want you to link to them! Because real estate professionals won't be able to stop this natural evolution (no matter how hard some of them try), it is better to accommodate it than fight it. Better yet, be a part of it!

Comparative Market Analysis Tools

In our opinion, the online comparative analysis tool has single-handedly upped the ante for online real estate. Just wait until Generation Y starts investing!

The key to comps is to find out what other homes in a neighborhood with similar square footage have sold for. This information is important to sellers, because many loans have appraisal and loan contingencies, meaning the buyer can back out of the deal with no financial loss if the home does not appraise at the purchase price or the buyer can't get a loan, again dependent upon the appraisal. Pricing a home correctly is also critical to attracting buyers fast and selling it quickly. If you want to look up these analyses, check out HomeSeekers.com (*http://homeseekers.com*) and Domania.com (*http://domania.com*). Another valuable tool is Home Price Check (*http://homepricecheck.com*), and yet another is RealEstateJournal. com (*www.realestatejournal.com/toolkit/homevalues/*).

Zillow.com also offers price analyses online for free. Many real estate professionals, when asked about this, said that they didn't want people to see the Zillow.com numbers because they were unrealistic, especially in a buyers' market. This may be the case, but in our opinion, it is better to offer the tool and then explain why it is unrealistic than to let the sellers find it on their own and feel as though you withheld the truth from them.

Some of these tools don't give the data right away, instead asking the visitor to fill out a form for an agent to contact them. Of the many tools for pricing, Domania.com is by far our favorite. To date, we have not received any unsolicited email from this company after using their tools.

Zillow Effect?

Don't ignore the data provided by Zillow.com, either. It is becoming an increasingly important player in the market and has incredible expertise at its helm. We realize that many real estate professionals disagree with the manner by which sites like Zillow.com arrive at their information, but the bottom line is that their methods may not matter. If enough consumers use Zillow.com to obtain home values, then you may see actual values gravitating towards the Zillow.com model rather than the other way around—and no appraiser in the world will be able to do anything about it. Not to mention, your sellers and buyers will use it to gauge your effectiveness and determine if you are being transparent with your information. You may wish to go as far as to say, "While Zillow says this, this is reality based on X, Y, and Z."

Zillow.com has just stepped things up a bit by entering the home sales arena. Technologists and those wanting a more level playing field love this! This is a new venture for Zillow.com but appears to have potential, at least early on. The *Los Angeles Times* published an article entitled "Zillow Is for Sales, Not Just Snooping," which described the impact that this new offering may have on the "traditional system." According to the article, Zillow.com became an overnight success by allowing homeowners to find out quickly and easily how much their houses, and those of their neighbors, were worth. Now Zillow.com will help owners let everyone know how much they want for their homes. Homeowners can now use Zillow.com to post virtual "For Sale" signs for free. Zillow contains a database of over 60 million homes, yet until now, it wasn't possible to find out which ones were for sale.

Some analysts believe that the traditional system of buying and selling homes may be threatened. According to one industry consultant, "[Buying and selling homes online] is just one more chink in the armor of the established brokerage industry. It provides consumers with more choices."

It is still unknown how successful this new venture will be, as there is so much competition on the Internet. The number one site is still REALTOR.com®, which offers one of the largest collections of for-sale listings. Other companies, like RE/MAX, are starting to offer online listings, and only time will tell what the future has in store for the more traditional sites.

Online listings are a great way for Zillow.com to make users come back to the site again and again. It will take a while, however, to populate enough for-sale listings in the system to provide users with an accurate picture of the market. Zillow.com is depending on sellers to populate the listings voluntarily, as it will not be drawing information from the multiple listing service.

Richard Barton, the cofounder of Zillow.com, has a great track record. He is the creator of Expedia and has applied basically the same formula to Zillow.com, providing consumers with access to information previously controlled only by agents. Will the impact that Zillow.com has be as deep as that of Expedia on the travel industry? That remains to be seen.

Barton does not believe that agents will be eliminated, but there may be downward pressure on fees, or, at the very least, agents will need to work harder to justify their commissions. There are already many "success stories" of individuals selling their homes on their own with the help of Zillow.com.

Sellers using Zillow.com can work with or without brokers to set a price and post the traditional photos and descriptions. They can even link to other sites and communicate with potential buyers through email. An icon of a flag on the Zillow.com community map designates that a particular home is for sale. Real estate agents are already posting their listings on the site. The Make Me Move feature lets buyers who aren't anxious to sell name a price that will literally "make them move." Even if the feature isn't very useful (though homes have been sold this way), it is fun—one element that attracts people to sites like Zillow.com, along with curiosity.

As popular as Zillow.com has become, it has yet to turn a profit. It makes its money selling advertising. The more traffic to the site, the more money the company can charge for its advertising space.

Choose Partners Carefully

Be careful whom you partner with. If you link to a company or a service industry that does not have a good reputation with consumers, its reputation will reflect poorly on you. This is especially true for mortgage brokers, who are in general receiving a bad name, particularly within the investment community. Analyze tools before recommending them and read what others have to say before just posting a link. Better yet, let others in your blog talk about which tools you provided that were of most help and listen if they complain about a particular tool. That's another great thing about blogs: You're not really responsible if someone happens to post something that's not quite accurate. Sure, you check up on everything and post follow-ups when needed, but users know that blogs are open forums that are susceptible to occasional inaccuracy. Nonetheless, don't forget to subscribe to your own blog so you can monitor activity. Too much incorrect information out there can make you look incompetent. With any technology that is consumer driven and consumer oriented, there is some need for follow-up and responsiveness.

4 Attract Buyers for Your Own Listings

ONE KEY ELEMENT to making money in real estate is attracting buyers for your own listings. This gives you the entire commission rather than having to split it with the buyer's agent. Think about selling yourself, your business, and the value that you bring, not the listings that you put up. Listings will come and go, so it makes sense to focus on you and your business and what you bring to the table—not your listings, which will change in a month.

As counterintuitive as this might seem, try thinking of yourself as a for-sale-by-owner client. As FSBO sellers themselves, the authors know the mind-set full well. FSBOs know what is appealing about their home and have a specific time frame in which to sell it, so they are often aggressive sellers. As FSBOs, we don't sit back and wait. We hold our open houses, we post our homes at Zillow. com, we put our homes in the MLS, we get them up on FSBO sites and Craigslist—you name it, we do it! In fact, in our experience, we've been more invested and aggressive in our own real estate sales than our agents. Try to think like the FSBO sellers, take every sale very seriously, and mount an aggressive campaign to get top-dollar offers. After all, someone who chooses to sell their home with an agent is paying more to do so. They may full well be getting more service, but they are paying a lot of money (especially on pricey homes). Bringing in offers that are less than decent to get the house closed isn't acceptable to FSBO clients. They expect top dollar; in fact, they are paying top dollar for the best! Try to get into this mind-set as you write and create your sites.

Try selling aggressively and selling quickly. What would you do if you had a month or six weeks to sell the home, period? What if it was *your* home, and you were selling by owner? Looking at things from this perspective may encourage a new style of campaign. Some of you already do this, and we commend you (and you are the type of agent we like working with!) but many don't, and we've seen it firsthand ourselves. Obviously, anytime you sell your own listing, you make more money. Hopefully, you are performing so well that you're also creating repeat clients.

Selling Your Own Listings with Technology

So how do you sell your own listings using technology? Consider video blogs. You can easily host them and make money. A video blog or a podcast featuring a tour of a property or even the local area could be inspiring to potential buyers. If they aren't already represented by an agent, they will be more likely to call you. Obviously, you can get a greater commission by representing both parties. For video blog features, look at the Google Video Blog site (*http://googlevideo.blogspot.com*). For another great example, check out Vlog System (*www.netartmedia.net/vlogsystem*) and the demo that goes along with it at *http://modellprojekt.com*.

Blogging Your Way to Buyers

You can incorporate blogs into your existing website so that you have synergy and consistency throughout your branding efforts. In fact, we recommend this strategy; it will create an automatic lead to your website if someone visits your blog and vice versa. To be effective, a blog should be a featured aspect of your website. Don't position it in the same way as you would a "comments" section. In other words, it should not be an afterthought or a component of your website that someone goes to after having exhausted all the other pages. Actually, many complete websites out there are blogs; in other words, the entire website is a blog. The authors don't recommend this approach for a real estate agent, but it illustrates the power and faith people have in blogs.

Real Estate Professional Blog

One of the most popular real-estate-specific blogs—which we highly recommend and use to host our own blog—is RealTown Blogs (*www.realtownblogs.com*). The founders of this blog, the team at InternetCrusade.com, are well regarded as movers and shakers in the real estate technology world. On the website, CEO Saul Klein lists his top ten blog tips. We are so enthusiastic about his advice, we thought we'd share it here:

1. *Understand what a blog can do for you.* Blogs are frequently updated and blend personal opinions and fact with links to other resources. If done right, your blog will showcase your real estate know-how and differentiate you from other practitioners in your market.

2. *Determine the purpose of your blog.* Before you leap into the world of blogging, find your focus. Your blog can be professional, fun, or educational or any combination of those. Define your blog's goal. Will it position you as the neighborhood real estate expert? Will it service your clients and prospects? Will it help you network with other real estate pros or with fellow hobbyists?

3. *Select blog software.* There's no shortage of programs that make it extraordinarily simple to create and update a blog. With no more effort or time than it takes to compose an email, you can have your latest blog entry up on the Web. Experiment with different software programs, such as Google's Blogger or InternetCrusad's RealTown Blogs, both of which are free.

4. *Address the needs of your target audience.* Think of yourself as an editor who must provide compelling and relevant news and filter information on your audience's behalf. For example, if your audience is primarily buyers, use your blog to deliver buying tips and information on properties just minutes after they hit the market.

5. *Update your blog regularly.* Create a schedule of when you'll add new postings, whether it is three times a day or once a week. Let readers know how often the site is updated, then stay true to your word. Fresh content will keep your audience interested and will help the blog rank higher on search engines.

6. *Encourage audience participation.* Ask for opinions and feedback on the issues you cover in your blog—for example, "Which architectural style do you like best?" or "What would you like to see developed at the corner of Main Street and Forest Drive?" Also include a "comments" section where readers can post other feedback any time.

7. *Jazz it up.* Add dimension to your blog with photos, videos, and links to news articles, relevant websites, and your favorite blogs.

8. *Use RSS feeds.* A technology called RSS, short for "really simple syndication," allows you to distribute your blog content proactively. It works like this: People who visit your blog—and have already installed an RSS reader on

their computer—can click on a link you provide to have the content delivered straight to their reader. Make sure your blog software has RSS feed capability.

9. *Arrange postings by categories.* Your blog software will automatically sort your postings on your blog site with the newest content on top. But that makes it difficult for visitors to your site to zero in on the topics they find most interesting. Use the "categories" feature of your blog software to organize your postings by topic.

10. *Promote your blog at every opportunity.* Create a prominent link to the blog on your website, include the blog's Web address in your email signature, and reference your blog in all advertising and marketing materials. If you publish an article in your blog that you're particularly proud of, send a link to everyone in your sphere of influence. Be sure to have someone check your spelling and grammar before you publish. Errors will reflect badly on you.

To give you some examples of what quality blogs look like, check out the winners of the 2007 REBA awards. We list them in Appendix B, and we give you our own critique of each one.

You can easily see that blogs are becoming a mainstream technology in a real estate professional's arsenal to promote listings and to bring business in the door. Take a look at the specific sites we list in Appendix B and determine what you see as distinctive and creative about them. Also, check out InternetCrusade.com and its blogs at *http://blogs.internetcrusade.com.*

Best Blogging Bits

So how specifically can you use blogs to attract buyers? First, the blog can help establish you as a professional in the marketplace. Your presence in the online community will be greater with an active blog than without one. A key here is to be active; you need to participate frequently, offer added value, and let your community be part of your development efforts. Take control of your blog. You know the direction you want your business to go, so you need to steer your blog that way as well. Klein notes that bloggers should think of themselves as tour guides in the online world. He also notes that each blog's purpose must be clearly noted, and the authors have found it exceptionally important to stay on track. If you find tangents occurring, that may be good; after all it is a sign of activity. Consider creating separate blogs for those content areas so you maintain control. If the purpose of your blog is to discuss a community, pricing structures, the general real estate industry, or to get feedback, then be sure that you clearly state your purpose and try to keep the blog on track.

Be sure as the host of the blog that you log in regularly and update content. No one wants to be part of a blog in which the last entry is a month old! Refreshing content also helps search engines find you, another tip from Mr. Klein. It is highly recommended by the authors and InternetCrusade.com that you offer a comments area. People like to offer their opinions on a topic. Don't take offense at a difference in opinion; healthy debate is great for all parties. Be sure to remove offensive material quickly though, as such content will rapidly degrade the quality of your blog.

There are lots of additional features you can add. Klein specifically notes links, photos, video, permalinks (a unique URL for each posting), and blogrolls (links to your favorite fellow bloggers or blogs). The more options and flexibility you offer, the greater your blog's appeal to your audience.

You should use the RSS feeds we mentioned to help bring in buyers. This will help push your information out to those interested parties. Klein has an example of this strategy up at *http://blog.saulklein.com*. Arranging your posts by category will help keep your content organized and will help minimize confusion for the viewer or blogger. You can also use sticky entries, keeping particularly interesting or informative blog posts at the top or in the order you choose for people to refer to easily. This is especially useful for content-rich posts, but be sure to use it with discretion. Too many stickies can be overwhelming.

Be sure to promote your blog at every opportunity. Think of how many emails you send in a day. Why not make your blog's URL part of your signature? Create links to it from your website. Find out if the companies you partner with would allow you to post a link or do it for you. Participate in others' blogs and post your blog information in your signature line. Ask other bloggers to blogroll you.

If you want a free blog and you want one immediately, take a look at *www.realtownblogs.com*. InternetCrusade.com will create one immediately for you for free. Click the "Create Your Own" link and have at it! Also, take a look at companies that are dedicating themselves specifically to the real estate market. One to consider is Transparent Real Estate Technologies (*http://transparentretech. com*). This company promises to help you market and blog your way to success in the real estate world.

Here's something else we found very relevant in Klein's information—we've seen it ourselves firsthand—someone online somewhere is always wanting to pick a fight with you. We've seen it at Amazon. com and in personal email—the more you put yourself out there, the more open to critique and criticism you become. Don't feel too offended when bad feedback comes your way; although the first time is a bit of a punch to the gut, it is inevitable. Eventually you will thicken your skin. While we've never become "accustomed" to it, nor do we think getting used to it is possible unless you are a big-time public figure or politician, you do learn to minimize its impact.

Make friends online—link to business partners and colleagues. Everyone likes to feel a part of the "in" crowd and the network. You are portraying your connections through your site more than just your words. Remember that you are selling an image of yourself. What image is your site portraying? Not sure? Ask people! Marketers do this all the time through focus groups, and so should you.

Also, realize that search engines aren't going to find you auto-matically. While they do crawl (search for sites by following links from other sites), it's important you build meta tags, data about data, into your site, your blog, and anything else you put out there. It is your job to put yourself in the search engines, either through the hundreds of third-party tools available or through using meta tags. Don't stack your website with an endless array of terms that you feel will give it better placement; search engines aren't that eas-ily fooled! Rather, limit your meta tags to only the terms that you feel best describe your business. Also, remember that some of the sites you find online and the blogs you participate in will be chock-full of people who can give you referrals. ActiveRain is a great social networking site for real estate professionals that can actually lead to business. Don't be led astray by other peoples' blogs or sites; just focus on what you do best. Don't get sidetracked by interest-ing conversations that may create controversy not good for you. Everywhere you turn, someone will be competing for airtime, for the prominent opinion, to be the first to predict something—this is all irrelevant to you. Just focus on what you want your blog and your site to be and go for it.

Enhance Your Online Services—Represent the Buyer and Seller

Many real estate pros have been using virtual tours and lots of photos for a few years. In fact, the numbers clearly show that not having a virtual tour up can immediately turn off a potential homebuyer, so you want to be sure to offer as much visual com-munication at initial contact as possible to bring buyers to you. Some buyers will look for homes themselves, then simply phone the listing agent rather than having their own agent represent them. This critical development is one major way that the Internet has impacted real estate. Yet, promoted properly, it can be an excellent way for you to increase your business potential.

We are not advocating removing virtual tours or photos but rather enhancing the such content-rich information. In Chapter 1, we discussed using podcasts or video podcasts to provide a thorough commentary about the home. What about also showcasing you and your practice in a video podcast? Consider producing videos about you and your business and what you offer buyers. Talk about the seamless relationship you create between the seller of a home you represent and the potential buyer, should that buyer decide to contact you directly. This is a great way to become the agent for both parties. Your technology may even help you take listings from FSBO sellers, when they see what you can offer.

Wilmington Realcast (*http://wilmingtonrealcast.com*) is a real-estate-specific video podcasting company. A *realcast* is a real estate podcast. Listings are submitted and then compiled into a podcast that is usually 12 to 15 minutes long. While Wilmington Realcast is only offering one episode per week, the company will be expanding. For real estate agents, realcasts are marketed locally, and we know how important this is—perhaps the number one factor in your success and recognition in the marketplace. Wilmington Realcast also allows you to customize audio and video podcasts for your own website so that site visitors won't need to leave your site to get material. The company has gone as far as to offer what we are recommending in this book—video podcasts as the next phase of virtual tours. Realcast will let you record the seller's thoughts on the property and the agent's thoughts and sales pitch, do voiceovers, and walk buyers through listings.

Your Web Site—"Content Rich" Can Make You Rich!

Your website is probably the key element of your online presence. Generally speaking, the more content-rich information you have, the better. Of course, too much of anything can become counterproductive, so you have to find the balance that works for you and your clients. Some people do not want to receive a follow-up phone call in response to an email message; they want to receive an email response. It is important to understand what these individuals want and adjust your technology accordingly. Internet-savvy people want information right at their fingertips; they don't want to have to hear a voice sales pitch to get information, and they don't want to feel pressured. They want to put the potential home on the "look at" or "do not look at" list immediately without having to talk on the phone, so offer up lots of information about your listings. Create the blog for the community. Create a virtual tour, a podcast, a video—everything you can to provide as much information as possible. While you're at it, create an opportunity for the viewer to get more information *by email* by providing their email address via a Web link. You can then follow up, find out more about what the buyer is seeking, and possibly create a new client.

The authors recommend using a program called Constant Contact for email marketing. You can download a trial copy from *www.constantcontact.com*. A post called "The Power of Email" in ActiveRain provided some great information and insight into this topic (Kruse, 2006). The author recommended an email list and over time built it up tremendously. The author used a team approach to do this, asking every contact to join the mailing list. Business partners did the same. While you may only add a few people here or there, eventually you can add people you find at trade shows, through colleagues and referrals, from business cards you pick up, etc., and your list will grow tremendously.

The power of email is incredible. Once you start networking, the process is what we call *viral*. That is, for every one person who knows five more who may be interested, the numbers multiply in an exponential manner. Before you know it, you have a huge list. Of course, due to legal requirements, you must offer an opt-out (and you must take out the names in accordance with the law!), but email is a powerful tool regardless. If you aren't continually sending spam, we've found that most people choose to stay on the list.

5 Attain Record Sales

ACHIEVING RECORD SALES in any industry requires several successful components to come together seamlessly: a fabulous reputation, an outstanding marketing campaign, a top-notch product or service, and great communication. Strong sales will give you greater negotiating room with your brokers or representatives and help you retain the best partners possible for your clients—and that advances your reputation for providing the best service. It will also help you retain clients in less-than-stellar market conditions, about which we'll talk more later. You already know many ways to provide excellent service, but is your technology also providing the best service? Are you providing detailed information, easy contact queries, updates, community forums, and videos for the people who visit your site? If not, now is the time to begin.

Using Cookie-Cutter Sites

Cookie-cutter websites may not always allow you to take full advantage of the Internet's marketing potential. According to a recent NAR survey, 72 percent of buyers use the Internet to search for homes, and some surveys suggest this number is higher than 80 percent. One thing is clear—everybody's doing it. Twenty percent of buyers first discovered their home through the Internet. These numbers can't be ignored because they will certainly grow.

Investing in an effective website is money well spent. A big reason is that buyers who use the Web to find their homes tend to be wealthier and spend more. In fact, buyers who find their homes on the Web spend an average of $452,000, as compared to $310,000 for homes found using traditional methods. This is close to 50 percent more—meaning 50 percent more in commissions! If that's not enough, a survey by the California Association of REALTORS® concluded that Internet buyers took half as much time to find and buy their homes as those who didn't use the Internet. This quick turnaround is due to the legwork that the Internet buyers perform on their own, a testament to the time-saving advantages of the Web.

The most surprising and somewhat counterintuitive statistic is that Internet buyers are more likely to use a real estate agent to complete their transaction! You may have thought that those who prefer to use the Internet are looking for ways to avoid an agent, but apparently that's not the case.

We found some great advice on websites and what works for real estate agents at Realty Times® (*http://realtytimes.com*), an outstanding resource. The advice is very much in line with our suggestions in the previous chapters. Look at the websites and blogs we mention. What do you like, and what don't you like? What message is being communicated? Did the website distract its visitors? What did *you* as the visitor find distracting? What did you find appealing? What did you automatically gravitate towards? Was your gravitation due to the site or your own interests? How did you find the site? Will you return? Why? How did you bookmark the site? Did it give you an option to bookmark it through a tool on the site? What about making it your home page? Was the message supportive or overwhelming? Did the site load fast? Did you get a sense immediately of what the site owner was all about, and was the site's message clear?

Technically Savvy Consumers and the Web

In our interviews with tech-savvy Gen Xers and Yers, we found that they want as much information as possible to be provided electronically. In fact, most don't even want to talk to a real estate professional until they are ready to see the home, and even then, they wouldn't mind being given a key that works for an hour to check out the property on their own without your commentary. This is what you are up against: Technology-smart people take matters into their own hands and prefer self-service. They are asked to go it alone by just about every other industry, and many younger Americans have become so comfortable and self-reliant that they avoid traditional face-to-face services.

How does your business fit in? Do you give people the tools they need to make a decision, which in turn highly qualifies leads before they come to you? It may seem as though you are getting fewer leads this way; yet what you are actually doing is getting less administrative overhead and more highly qualified leads. Offer them comparative analyses. Provide maps with overlays of restaurants, railroad tracks, and airports. Provide listings of other homes in their search area that may interest them. Provide a video log of the home tour. Offer a virtual tour and a podcast from the seller. Give them lots of information on the community, the schools, crime rates, demographics—everything they need to determine if an area is right for them. If they have all of this information and they phone you, you have a highly qualified lead. It is better to spend your time on serious buyers and sellers than to waste it answering questions that clients can easily answer on their own online. Believe it or not, most prefer to get information online.

To monitor your sales, make certain you're following up as appropriate. Make sure that leads don't go unanswered; you need to have a system on your *back end* (we didn't coin that term!) dedicated to managing all of this. Technologists refer to the *back end* as the driving force that runs a system but that the user doesn't see. What the user sees is called the *user interface.* Some real estate pros use a simple spreadsheet to help them track leads; others use a database or a standard real estate leads software. Whatever you decide to use, spend time each day keeping on top of your list and maintain traditional sales techniques even while using technology. Technology does not entirely replace old models, but it certainly enhances them. You can even do this all online with various products.

If about 80 percent of homebuyers are using the Internet in their search for a home, you can use this knowledge to achieve record sales by providing stellar information and interacting frequently with your online community. Check out ListingDomains. com (*http://listingdomains.com*), which grew 600 percent in 2006. The company provides individual property websites to real estate professionals looking to compete with the big guys. Other organizations with a similar business model are out there, too, so you're sure to find one that fits nicely with your requirements—and your budget. The nice thing about ListingDomains.com is that each property gets its own Web address. For example, a property at 555 Main Street will have an address of *www.555MainStreet.com,* providing information specific to that listing. Many top real estate professionals in the country are using this tool to achieve record sales numbers, making this method worth investigating.

Web Integration

Remember throughout your website offerings that your solutions, your services, and your blogs and Web content must all be integrated. One of the keys to a successful Web 2.0 deployment (or dynamic website effort) is to be certain that each tool relates to and works seamlessly with the rest. Take comments and suggestions seriously and ask others to critique your site for obvious holes you may have missed in development. Unless you use a canned product, chances are you aren't going to handle the development effort yourself, so be sure to communicate your marketing and business-oriented needs to Web developers. Often, Web techies are focused on development and coding and not business strategy and modeling—that's your job. Communicate frequently and regularly, ask your community for its opinions and feedback through a comments section on your website, and don't get defensive over unhappy consumers or dissatisfied bloggers. Some negative feedback is to be expected but overall will increase your visibility. Address problems or issues promptly, and you'll keep many satisfied customers.

Technological Change—Contributing Factors

To step back a bit, we should examine several of the building-block technologies that have led consumers and providers to the Web 2.0 revolution.

High-Speed Internet Access

Affordable high-speed Internet access—even in remote areas—has provided many home computers the ability to search the Internet as quickly as their counterparts in offices and schools. In the "old days," people had to go to work if they wanted to surf the Web fast. Today, a cable connection can net a connection rate of five MB per second—three times faster than that of a company with a T1 line!

As a result of the high bandwidth availability in homes and businesses, content-rich presentations can easily be downloaded. These may include numerous high-quality (therefore large-file-size) photos, virtual video tours, and brochures in PDF format that are viewable on any platform. While the digital divide (the growing disparity between the haves and have-nots regarding Internet access) is leaving a sector of the market outside the Internet, this gap is becoming smaller as more individuals than ever have access.

Online Searching

Search agents have had a considerable impact on the ability to look for data and provide reliable information on the Internet. Google, Yahoo!, MSN, and Ask together make up a majority of the searching market, with Google capturing most of the market share. Now it is easy to find an appraiser, for instance, in Austin, Texas, by simply typing in *appraiser Austin*. Today, Google Base is making its mark on the industry as well. Google Base lets you describe an item or a service with or without a website. You can submit all types of content into Google Base to make the information searchable. Data can pop up into Google Maps, Google Web search, and Google Products search. You can also add attributes to content to make it more easily searchable and also more relevant to the searcher. Visit *http://base.google.com* to enter information and begin. For low or no cost, anyone can enter information directly into Google Base.

Extensible Markup Language, commonly known as XML, is a technical term for determining how data is defined. The industry has agreed on Document Type Definition, known as DTD, as the standard for listing data and property information so it will appear the same on any platform or within any Web browser, regardless of where it is hosted. This code has created numerous possibilities for searching any source on the Internet, including nationwide MLSs. Local real estate agents must have a broker's license in the area (or state) where they want to subscribe to an MLS and then pay an MLS subscription fee. With nationwide Internet searching, one of the advantages agents had in finding property has been eliminated.

Today, we see Asynchronous JavaScript (AJAX) leading the way in development methodology for creating interactive application—

critical to Web 2.0 development efforts. Web pages feel more responsive when they exchange data with the server behind the scenes so that the page does not have to be reloaded each time the user makes a change. This functionality increases the interactivity level with the user, the speed of the page, and its overall usability; it is also a standard that conforms to Web 2.0.

It is critical to explain "why AJAX?" at this point in the book, because when you begin to work with a Web developer or architect, you'll need to understand their development methods and solutions. AJAX and Reverse AJAX impact the time it takes the users of your site to interface with it. Who wants to wait forever for a page to load? If clients have to wait, they may leave. Using AJAX and Reverse AJAX reduces the number of times the page has to pull or push data to the users of the website. Web designers need to use this type of code. Whatever programming language used (the most popular are SP and PHP, but JSP and ColdFusion are also frequently used), your Web developer should be embracing this technology. AJAX can be embedded with the other types of programming methods.

The Web 2.0 Design Process

Some would argue that perhaps above all else, your Web designer or developer needs to understand the needs of your site visitors. Some look to Web developers as programmers, and you can do that if you will be the content expert. However, it's helpful to work with someone who understands both the technical and business side of your website. Web usability is a key indicator of the designer's ability to develop for your clients.

Good Web architects will build a website much like a house, first making a blueprint, then constructing the home. This blueprint should lead to a prototype of the site that you will want to test with potential clients. Don't ask other real estate professionals (unless they are your audience)—ask the people who would be using the site! Play an active role in the design as well. Don't just hand over the Web development effort and then ignore it until it is done. The more dynamic websites become and the more content and information they deliver in distinctive and changing ways, the more important the selection of your Web architect. A good architect will do a usability study (making sure the site is usable by the intended visitors) and build a website that is engaging, interactive, user-friendly, and useful. Many will be happy to do a pilot study for you—you cannot find out unless you ask.

Portability

One thing to remember about websites is that they need to be "portable." This means that they should be interpreted the same way across various browsers and versions of these browsers. A standard called World Wide Web Consortium (W3C) is a compliance requirement for valid Web programming code. Using W3C means that the website you create would be accessible by a greater viewing audience, because no matter what the user's circumstance, the site will be visible the same way. W3C refers to its process as "validating Web documents in formats like HTML and XHTML for conformance to W3C recommendations and other standards." Not meeting W3C compliance can jeopardize the website's potential to be successful and draw the maximum number of visitors. Adhering to this standard is not for cosmetic reasons but for accessibility. Be sure that you visit *www.w3.org* and understand World Wide Web Consortium's compliance standards so that you can ensure your Web designer users the appropriate tools.

Your Web developer needs to know how to engage the viewer, convincing the viewer that the site personally *knows* them. This can be done with proper programming and good planning. Plain old HTML won't let you create a Web version 2.0 site that is fluid and usable. Flash and Shockwave may help, as may some other languages your Web developer may mention, including PHP, ASP, JavaScript, and ColdFusion. It is up to the Web developer/Web architect to decide which combinations of programming languages will create a special dynamic user/website interaction. What is important is that you understand the options and your priorities so you can communicate with the developer.

In Web terms, *behavior* is the interaction between user and website. Behavior personalizes the site in a way that most sites don't. The site gives the user opportunities, then actually responds to the user. Users get feedback in real time, and your site will be able to address the user by whatever method you choose—first name, log-in ID, location, etc. You can also use email links on Web pages so clients can contact you directly using their own email system without having to go through a form. In the former scenario, the developer programs the page to interact; in the second, the developer uses basic HTML to give the user something less dynamic and more static.

Avoiding Web Hazards

Be sure that you know the potential hazards of development and ask your developer for updates. In an interview with Cheryl Ann Henry, a professional Web architect with clients all over the nation, we asked her to name the top five potential "gotcha's" for Web development specific to real estate:

Q: *What are the top five (or more) hazards people run into when developing a dynamic website? What pitfalls as a Web architect would you advise they do their best to avoid?*

A: 1. **Forgetting to standardize on W3C.** Don't just build a website using a template or something that has code that cannot be interpreted the same way by every browser. Without W3C compliance, the user, given various browsers, browser versions, monitor display area settings, etc., experiences the website in different ways; not everyone gets a consistent look and feel or behavior for the website. The site should also be in valid XML, HTML, or CSS, etc. [Authors' note: While you can simply demand this of your developer, take a look at this website to understand more: *www.w3.org*.]

2. **Not taking advantage of the site to give it behavior.** The site can react and can actually act if it is designed to do so! *Behavior* also refers to how the website or Web application interfaces with the server when it comes to loading or reloading site pages. It can also refer to interaction with the users; it could refer in particular to the responses that it gives the users, as if it is communicating with them. [Authors' note: This is why it is important to hire someone who is experienced and understands the latest Web technology. In our opinion, this behavior is essentially the foundation of Web version 2.]

3. **Websites that don't engage the user.** Too much sophistication and technology can detract from the usability factor, which is important. Think of the highest-tech cell phone that makes it nearly impossible to dial numbers! It might look cool, but you'd prefer a phone that works. Websites must be easy to navigate, easy to use, user-friendly, and useful. They should be intuitive for people to use, not too intimidating. Remember that even very savvy people may become intimidated by technology and want things simple—minus the bells and whistles. [Authors' note: Don't let this advice keep you from linking to great sites that provide useful tools.] Another thing to keep in mind is that the site needs to be not "heavy." This means that it needs to load quickly and not be so inundated with items, graphics, downloads, etc., that

it provides for a poor user experience. Web developers need to understand that only about half the U.S. population has high-speed Internet. Websites can still look amazing yet be built for the lowest common speed denominator.

4. **Sites that use Flash are a big problem; Flash and Shockwave, both multimedia options, are ineffective uses of multimedia.** Find a way to involve the user directly so that if they do not have a plug-in, they can still use the site. Don't provide obstacles to get to the site (such as a Flash introduction). Flash on the site itself may distract the user from what you want them to focus on. What's better is a nice multimedia movie or a lead. You will get the lead when they fill out a form—either for a membership, a newsletter, feedback, support, or something—not from multimedia. You can generate interest in something, but if there is no follow-through after the interest is piqued, then it is pointless. [Authors' note: In our opinion, the same rule applies to websites that have the "High-Speed," "Non-High-Speed," "Flash," "Non-Flash" options when you first visit. Not only are they annoying, but you should have technology that isn't dependent on a download—or a pop-up that may be blocked!]

5. **Not securing the site.** Sometimes designers forget the value of securing transactions between the Web server and the browser. For example, when people are filling out forms or providing any type of personal information, you need to be sure you offer a secure transaction and let people know that you are securing it—make sure they know you care about their privacy. [Authors' note: Don't abuse email addresses that you collect! Keep private information private, unless the user agrees to let you share their

information with your partners.] Also, be sure you include a privacy statement that accurately reflects how and what you'll use their information for (or preferably that you don't use their info!). Be sure you have a "Security Terms and Conditions" area on your site as well. There are many standard ideas on just about any website, or you could go as far as to have an attorney write it up for you.

Critical Technology Integration

What are some additional ideas of features to include in your site? When working with your architect, be sure you're covering all of the bases—what does your client want?

Demographic information is imperative for investors and homeowners wanting to know more about the area into which they are moving or purchasing. This data is readily available now thanks to published information, government sites, and census data. Most counties publish websites with data on employment, for instance. Assessor offices publish tax information and data about parcels; even small towns without much infrastructure have incredible information available on liens, taxes, and about any data you could want on a piece of property. Some investors use this data to seek out homeowners who are severely behind on property taxes to make them a low offer on their home, pay off their taxes, and create a win-win situation.

This online data is making it easier to purchase the often-coveted foreclosures or bank repossessions that can make investors the most money. However, one major caveat that has held back the real estate profession is the risk that files can be tampered with. Electronic signatures were once considered insecure.

Just a few years ago, Adobe PDFs were a secure method of transmitting information. One could not easily modify a PDF, and it was relatively secure. Today, PDFs are easily modifiable with inexpensive software. However, Universal Forms Description Language, or UFDL, is becoming a new standard to create tamper-proof documents that preserve data and formatting. We still need to develop ways to sign these digitally and submit them electronically, but numerous companies are working on these problems, and this technology is one of the last pieces of the complete online transaction solution. Once it is mastered, we will see the use of technology explode in the real estate and financial markets.

Mapping and satellite imagery are another critical technology, providing neighborhood information and actual pictures of homes. Tools such as Google Earth and Microsoft's Maps (at *http://maps. live.com*) are revolutionizing the way we get data about potential home purchases. The consumer can add items like gas stations, airports, freeways, military bases, and other local features to these images to get a virtual, remote picture of what the area is like. As an agent, be aware of these tools and use them yourself. Provide them as a service from your site for your potential clients. The ability to overlay demographic data like schools, crime, community information, economic statistics, and addresses on a map make it even more useful. Zillow.com allows individuals to see a map of an area with comps and expected sales prices on top of it all! The comparative analysis models are still being refined for accuracy, but the system certainly has the makings of a technology revolution.

We know that technology integration is critical to the viability of technologically advanced real estate transactions, including those you will use on your own website. The coauthor of this book, Dani Babb, is the author of the book *Commissions at Risk*, which explains the coming technological age in the real estate business and the impact it will have on the marketplace. For instance, the ability to apply for and retain a mortgage online while being able to compare rates of multiple lenders by submitting one application is a tremendous asset to the homebuyer and investor. In addition, it is allowing individuals to create their own relationships with lenders, bypassing the one their agent has with a banker or broker and creating long-term partnerships based on trust and expediency. As systems become more secure, online payments will become less of a hassle and less worrisome. While most online transactions are protected, and consumers have been warned not to use nonsecure sites, some individuals still worry about conducting banking online. However, this concern is becoming less of an issue, as explained in detail in *Commissions at Risk.*

The inability to process complicated transactions has been another stumbling block for the real estate industry. As technology has advanced, however, information technology professionals have been increasingly motivated to understand business processes. Among the highest paid IT professionals are those who are business consultants; they frequently have MBAs. They have figured out how the complicated process of completing a real estate transaction can be completed successfully online. Some of the final barriers to this model were the ability to sign documents securely and notarize and electronically sign and file paperwork, which we discuss in the section on eclosing in Chapter 6. As more industries agree on data transmission standards, this functionality will become the norm, so understanding and monitoring it is critical. Your acceptance of this technology, sooner rather than later, is crucial.

Make Some Extra Dough Through Your Killer Site

There are lots of ancillary ways to make money online. Some Web designers and marketers advocate advertising on your site or allowing others to pay for click-throughs or leads. This is somewhat controversial to us, because while you may gain a few extra bucks (or even a few thousand extra bucks), you risk upsetting and frustrating your clients and consumer base. There is a fine line here between annoying ads and subtle ads, and the subtle ads usually don't make you a whole lot of money. Nonetheless, the question begs to be asked: If the ad is in good taste, why not post it and make some extra money? We are not suggesting you shouldn't, but weigh your options and choose carefully.

Perhaps a safer route is to create affiliate links to companies or people with whom you partner. Affiliate programs are usually some sort of advertising program that offers monetary compensation for webmasters to direct traffic to the advertiser's site. This is a win-win, because the advertisers get warm leads and the webmasters get a share in the profits from sales generated. There are lists of affiliates online; the ones you choose will depend on your particular line of business. You may wish to offer books on finding real estate in a particular location or mortgage information as an Amazon.com affiliate, for instance. Or you may wish to go after real-estate-based affiliates or even those offering seminars to educate clients.

After exhausting all of your partnerships, consider scouring the Internet for other partnerships related to real estate. Usually very little is involved in the affiliate network. For example, consider the Amazon.com affiliate link. As an affiliate, Amazon.com gives you the HTML code that you put right into your website, and up pops a link that automatically tracks when people came from your site and what revenue they generated for Amazon.com. Then, monthly, quarterly, or yearly, the affiliate will pay out the percent promised. Often, this is as little as 2 percent, but it can be as much as 20 percent! One site to look at is LinkShare™ (*http://linkshare.com*). This affiliate network operates very differently than an individual affiliate by bringing together organizations such as OfficeMax, Barnes and Noble, Lending Tree, Dell, and 800Flowers—this isn't just for the little guys! Linkshare manages your affiliate program for you. If you wish, you can pay the sites for click-throughs instead of leads that turn into sales, but doing so can get quite expensive.

Another option to generate ad revenue without seeming obvious to your clients is affiliate marketing. An affiliate is a partner organization with which you are affiliated in the traditional sense. You can partner with affiliate organizations, put a link from your site to theirs, and then ask them to do the same for you. In our opinion, it's best to find a way to integrate the link as a tool rather than an ad. Sometimes, you will be paid for click-throughs from your site; other times, you'll be paid based on actual revenue generated from your site. Consider offering a small amount of money for a lead generated from your affiliate, too. This is an important element to entice people to link to you. Consider area companies, vendors, partners you work with—ask them all for an online affiliate relationship (Henry, 2006).

Of course, to generate income from your website, people have to visit it. In fact, none of the advice we give in this book is of any practical value unless someone other than you actually uses your website, podcast, or blog! We've already discussed some ideas for you to generate traffic. Take a look at *www.youraffiliatecoach.com/ Website-Traffic.html* to see how to generate low-cost Web traffic. While the site is two years old, it has some great information that is still quite relevant today. Among the items we agree with is to exchange links. Make sure your site isn't a cul-de-sac! You want it linking to other sites, and you want those sites linking to you. Make it easy; put a "Link Together" section on your site and provide the HTML code for anyone to add you easily. If people ask you to add them, add them—unless, of course, you don't agree with their business practices or have a reason not to want to be affiliated with them. By exchanging links you also increase your hit rates in search engines.

Consider affiliate networking where you pay and get paid for those links and for click-throughs or buy-throughs. This strategy may be worth it. We use affiliate networking with Amazon.com and Barnesandnoble.com, for instance. If you are going to refer a site visitor to another organization and that person buys something, there is no reason for you not to be paid!

Also, we agree with the authors of YourAffiliateCoach—write articles where you can, especially for heavily visited sites. This will increase your exposure. Simply ask to have a link at the very bottom, perhaps linking your name to your website. Usually, most companies don't mind doing this, as the article benefits them. If they will let you include more data, have at it; consider writing a sentence or two about your business, your professional expertise, and how individuals may contact you. Also, be sure that you join others' forums and communities. You should join blogs and participate in forums that will make you better known and that represent your philosophy of business. We do not recommend becoming affiliated with a site that doesn't accurately represent your views, however. Whom we are linked with affects how others view us, whether we like it or not.

6 Generate Quick Closings

WOULDN'T IT BE fabulous to close a deal in two weeks? Technology makes it possible. By using Web version 2 and dynamic websites, a real estate professional can partner with escrow and title companies and set up esignings and even eclosings.

Adding Value the Technology Way

Here's a point that we cannot overstate: Some organizations are working diligently to "disintermediate" the real estate professional. What does this mean? Essentially, some believe that real estate professionals are middlemen who needlessly complicate or do not add value to real estate transactions. Some economists and many in the media are calling for drastic changes in the commission structure, deregulation, and Web-based solutions that eliminate the need for the real estate professional in all but the most complicated cases. In fact, some brokers online charge low commissions or a one-time flat fee to sell a home, and they're catching on quick. We know that you're already familiar with them. A *Los Angeles Times* article called "Low-Priced Brokerage Is Shaking Up Real Estate" featured one company, Catalist Homes (*http://catalisthomes.com*), whose published mission is "To reinvent the existing residential real estate business—an antiquated, inefficient, and costly system of selling homes."

A common belief today is that real estate professionals are over-compensated based on the service they provide. With home prices doubling and tripling, many people feel strongly that they should not pay the typical 5 to 6 percent commissions. Some homebuyers (and even some of our elected government officials) argue that real estate professionals are using anticompetitive practices and that commission rates didn't go up with inflation but rather with increasing home prices, which has been unfair to the consumer. Many companies are taking advantage of this new lower-cost or flat-fee market structure; Catalist Homes is one. It pays agents full-time salaries and then uses bonuses in a team model to help compensate for sales.

We have seen this low-cost and flat-fee commission structure happen in just about every other service industry as part of the process of disintermediation and price pressures. Industries as diverse as the diamond business to stock-trading companies and travel agents have felt the pressure. Many homesellers today don't have the needed equity in their homes, especially with the heavy foreclosure market, to sell with a real estate agent. Many, including the authors of this book, have sold homes on their own with great success, and while we are an exception to the rule today, we will not be a few years from now. This is one of many reasons you must get on the technology bandwagon today: to help market-proof your business! As technologists, we wish everyone in the real estate industry understood the amazing power of the Internet and the disintermediation and price pressures it is causing.

As the *Los Angeles Times* article indicates, and as we all know, many agents blackball listings. While this is not legal or ethical, we know that some agents simply will not show for-sale-by-owner homes that are "only paying 2 percent" (as Dani was told recently by a local agent). We know that even though the practice is dishonest, some agents still do not show homes listed by these flat-fee brokers. But think about this: As more and more clients come to you with a list of homes in hand that they already like, how are you going to convince them to stay away from these homes? We know most of you don't do it, but the few in the industry who do will wreak havoc for the rest of you.

Interestingly enough, the "test bed" for the nontraditional real estate agent for many of us was Catalist Homes in Hermosa Beach, nicely located in the South Bay area, a very hot area of the California marketplace. Keep an eye on it because some in the real estate business are arguing that this company is using anticompetitive practices. In September, the U.S. Department of Justice sued the National Association of REALTORS® over potential anticompetitive policies that kept costs artificially high and kept new competitors from joining the real estate industry and over MLS practices. NAR is defending itself, claiming that its policies are fair and that competition is good in the business.

As technologists, though, we've seen this happen often in the Internet age: Upstart companies or new industry paradigms are rebuffed by the existing business leaders. Eventually, the old guard succumbs to the pressure, and only the few who had the foresight to change with the times are remaining. Most people did not think 15 years ago that travel agents or stockbrokers would be paid a flat salary; today it happens all the time. Many articles compare stockbrokers to real estate agents, and this is a powerful statement for the industry as a whole. How many of us still go into a Merrill Lynch office or a Charles Schwab office? We may get advice from finance experts, often from television shows or online ratings, but we often make trades ourselves. Stockbrokers never imagined this would happen—that they'd work almost strictly with high-end and institutional investors.

Why should the real estate industry be any different? We are paid based on our ability to streamline processes, not to add more time-consuming and costly manpower to them. Inefficiency is our enemy! This is yet another reason why it is essential to embrace the technology available to you; companies like Catalist Homes are your *new competition*. Remember, too, it isn't only Catalist. Companies like For Sale By Owner.com, RealtyTrac® (great site for finding foreclosures online), Help-U-Sell® Real Estate, and ZipRealty are also changing the way real estate is handled.

For this book and *Commissions at Risk,* we studied all of the organizations noted above, and from what we can see as users of their products and service offerings, they are exceptionally well-run businesses and provide great power to the consumer for a very low cost. In fact, the authors listed their homes in the Multiple Listing Service (MLS), held their own open houses, put up a virtual tour, listed their homes at REALTOR.com®, and put lockboxes on their homes—all without the help of an agent. But would we consider a Web-savvy agent rather than the traditional ones we were stuck using? Probably.

Sites like Catalist Homes provide all the services of a real estate professional (including the marketing and advertising that comes with it) with lower fees. These sites are chock-full of people praising the sites, explaining how fantastic they were to use, how much money they saved, and how easy it was. As you develop your marketing campaign and take it onto the Web, keep these comments in mind. How do you offer full service, and why is your service better than that of a ZipRealty or a Catalist Homes? Are you going to blackball listings that offer a 1.5 percent commission rate, or will you embrace them, along with higher home prices, as a wave of the Internet future?

Remember that while your website may not overtly tell your clients that you are better than your new competitors, people who visit you online ought to understand this inherently without your having to state it explicitly. Herein lies the crux of the issue. When we bring up technology's risk to real estate professionals, we always hear the "service matters" stuff. While that is true (in fact, many companies, such as Nordstrom clothing stores, have built their entire brand around this notion), the low-cost real estate companies are still listing homes for half of what traditional agents are getting with service that many rate as just as good if not superior, especially in terms of responsiveness, to that offered by traditional models! Unless your particular niche is such that it simply cannot be replicated and your clients know it, you may unfortunately be relegated to being just another agent.

As you know, there has long been a protectionist attitude in real estate. Sellers offering only 1.5 to 2 percent were shunned unless buyers really wanted to see the house and they found it on their own. One of the obstacles that companies like Catalist Homes face is agents who won't look at their homes because they're offering half of the full commission rate. The authors have personally experienced this selling homes by owner. This protectionist approach may work in the short term, but in the long term, capitalism and consumerism always win out.

The information in the *Los Angeles Times* article is a testament that even hardened industry insiders have embraced technology. Check out the Catalist Homes site, and you will see many of the trends discussed and debated in real estate today. Not only flat-fee brokerage, but low-cost (3 percent) brokerage (stated right on their home page), the ability for individuals selling by owner to list their homes for free with Catalist Homes, the ability to search for homes for sale, and (as they say) a magnet for buyers and sellers—partially no doubt due to their unique model and easy-to-use site. From the seller's perspective, because the agents working for Catalist Homes aren't dependent upon the sellers' home prices for their paychecks, they have no incentive to sell homes for a low price just to reduce inventory or make a sale. Their agents earn a salary and a team bonus. Still not convinced this company is a powerful player? It focuses much of its effort on negotiation. For four straight years, it has had the highest listed home price to sale price (with 99.2 percent in 2004). It understands that a 3 percent commission today is equal to a 6 percent commission just a few short years ago because of the incredible increase in home values. Dollar for dollar, returns haven't changed much. Catalist Homes markets your home well, and because agents don't have to pay for the marketing themselves, they are given incentives and reason to market—not the other way around. Catalist Homes provides full advertising just like any other brokerage. It offers virtual tours, is in the MLS, posts homes on REALTOR.com®, holds a broker open house, hosts open houses for buyers, and stages the home. And it guarantees results!

So, you tell us—is online technology, like what Catalist Homes uses, a threat or an opportunity? Well, it can be either, depending on your perspective. However you feel about it, don't ignore technology or underestimate its growing influence. To be prepared for any potential risk, as a real estate professional you need to keep yourself acutely aware of what is happening in the market and what technological options are open to you. Be sure to partner with companies that embrace technology and see it not only as an advantage but also as a potential threat if not taken seriously enough.

Dynamic Sites to Help You Close Deals Faster

Let's get into some of the nuts and bolts of dynamic websites that can help you close sales faster. Take a look at E-Closing (*http://e-closing.com*). This website is for closers, processors, and lenders. The system works with agents, borrowers, sellers, lenders, and other organizations to complete the closing process online. As noted in *Real Estate News,* the entire process of eclosing takes about 13 minutes. Stewart Title Guaranty Company (*http://stewart.com*) is held in high regard for spending years perfecting the SureClose® and eClosingRoom™ services. Its system offers secure transactions and coordination as well as the useful ability to store all the title, deed, and loan information required to close a deal.

Secure websites require approval of documents, and then buyers are given an electronic pad to sign their signatures. Just one signature, and it is entered into all of the documents as appropriate for the transaction. Talk about a quick close! The Web system secures and encrypts digital signatures so they are legally binding. Stewart Title created the secure closing system; however, lenders must integrate with the system for it to work. As Internet technology becomes standardized in the mortgage business, expect systems like this to become mainstream and perhaps even expected by your buyers. Check out Fiserv (*http://fiservlendingsolutions.com*), another interesting developer of eclosing and emortgages that coordinates among lenders, agents, borrowers, sellers, and signing agents, all via the Web.

Let's face it, one of the valuable services that real estate agents have traditionally provided to clients has been to explain the mounds of paperwork containing legal mumbo jumbo. The bureaucratic process involved in buying or selling a home is quite intimidating to the average person. With increased automation, however, you may not be as needed as you once were. But that's all right—don't fight this automation. Embrace it and use it to your advantage by presenting it as a service that you offer that makes the entire process less painful for your client.

If you use a system that is automated, you will become known in your area for being easy to work with, fast, and efficient. You can even explain what you do and how you do it in a weblog or a podcast on your website. You save buyers an incredible amount of time and perhaps minimize potential closing problems. There are lots of solutions out there, so be sure to get references before selecting one.

Who's Looking for Your Web Systems?

It is imperative that any real estate professional understands the differences in generational requirements and demands from various industries. For instance, a 20-something will, generally speaking, be more inclined to demand Web applications than an 80-year-old. Understanding cultural changes and cohort expectations are crucial to implementing the right technology for your market. A quick review of some of the important elements that help define them may be useful for integrating your technology solution with your potential clientele.

The Generation Gap

Comfort with online transactions is helping drive change in the way real estate transactions are handled. Future generations will expect you to be able to handle transactions electronically. This is especially true for investors who don't have as much emotionally invested in a home purchase as, say, a first-time homebuyer or seller or someone looking to build a life somewhere. As generations grow up learning to use the mouse before going to preschool, this trend will continue, and professionals should be worrying. Statistics show that the generation you were born into dramatically impacts how "safe" you feel about the Internet as a place to conduct business. As younger generations have a greater impact on the market, their interest and demand for easier and efficient transaction will only increase.

Comfort Factor

More individuals are comfortable with technology today than ever. Financial companies are backing consumers if they get taken advantage of online, leading to an added feeling of security with online transactions. Consumers are aware of the relatively positive statistics associated with Web-based security and are more willing to trust a secure online environment because it is easier and more efficient for them. This comfort level creates an environment where many consumers feel little risk providing sensitive data to a trusted site through their keyboard.

Real Estate As an Investment

Many real estate transactions today involve the buying and selling of homes for investment purposes—a full quarter of all transactions, in fact. Individuals or institutional investors are largely looking for greater returns and a more stable environment than the stock market has been able to provide in recent years. While both markets move in cycles and are always subject to change, historically low interest rates, high consumer confidence, low unemployment, and higher incomes are allowing people to take more risk with their investments. Another factor is the popularity of securing a negative amortization loan with as little as 5–10 percent down! Many television shows geared towards business have featured professionals who note that real estate is a great way to get something tangible for investment dollars. Because of low interest rates, many are turning to homes to grow their nest eggs; some are even doing so in place of their traditional retirement savings. Many are turning to real estate to make highly leveraged investments, and this change is fueling the fire for Web-based transactions.

What does all of this mean? It is a reality check on what is driving the need for technology. Our culture is changing, and as people become more comfortable with technology, their expectations of you, the real estate professional, will change.

Podcasts and Closing Deals

It may be hard to imagine the relevance of podcasts to closing deals. But how much instruction must you give your buyers and sellers throughout the process, especially right before closing, on what to expect, how much time to allocate, when to move, etc.? How much of this information can you repeat from client to client? Now before you assume that no one in their right mind would prefer to listen to you tell them what to expect during closing while they're sitting at their computer in their pajamas at 2:00 AM, consider this: Why are universities embracing the idea of "lectures anytime," or asynchronous environments? Why are so many people putting French lessons or novels or business advice on podcasts? People no longer fit into a 9-to-5 job mold. They are used to working virtually, from anywhere, anytime that suits them. The information you give does not need to be delivered in person. In fact, many of us would prefer the opportunity to fast-forward through the parts we already know.

Before you dismiss this idea, consider a trial. Put your closing instructions on the Web. Ask your savviest sellers or buyers to view the podcast and then ask them what they thought. You can always still have a Q&A in person or even repeat the entire thing if they didn't like it. But we're confident that a particular segment of your market will be thankful they didn't have to schedule a 6:00 PM in-home meeting with you to get information about a process that, quite frankly, isn't "scary" to them anymore.

7 Showcasing Your Area Expertise

YOU ARE UNDOUBTEDLY an expert in your particular community and know everything about local news, the people, the culture,
the good, and the bad. But how well does the community know
you? Are you known as *the* area expert? If you are, you can use
technology to maintain that position. If you aren't, you can use
technology to help you get there.

You have firsthand insight into the community that you represent. So why are people going to sites that span the entire globe, like
Google Earth, for demographic information instead of counting on
you? Your information needs to be centralized and accessible on a
Web 2.0 platform that provides seamless, trusted access to all facets
of your expertise.

Tools for Showcasing Your Expertise

An abundance of tools for showcasing your expertise is available
online for just about every profession. Real estate is catching up
with the rest of the market. So what are some tools that you should

consider? Below you'll find a few. What you ultimately incorporate into your site depends on your audience, the type of service you want to offer, and your niche. But there are also some good general tools you should be aware of that may be useful to you, which we list in the "General Tools" section in Appendix B.

One of the objectives here is to get your site's visitors to fill out a profile to get access to various parts of the site (you need this information for marketing), so don't give away everything without registration. Be sure your site knows who they are, greets them by first name when they log in, and really gives them the contact that they want.

Webinars

Webinars are another great way to educate your base of consumers or clients and to create informative and interesting interactive tools that can be viewed anytime. Webinars are essentially Web-based seminars. They are used for everything from a large company presenting annual results to shareholders to a small business owner talking about accounting practices. We used to hear webinars referred to as Web conferencing. The only difference is that today they're much more sophisticated and even easier to use!

There are two main types of webinars. One is synchronous, meaning that your viewers need to be online at the same time as you. Another is asynchronous, which means that your viewers can view the webinar anytime they like, whether you happen to be online or not. We're fans of the asynchronous type, because you can create community centers to allow visitors to discuss the content but you don't need to be sitting at your computer at the time. More importantly, your visitor isn't restricted to particular times. You can even take the video and post it on YouTube or another video-sharing service. Web conferences tend to be synchronous, whereas webinars can be either. Usually they encompass both video and voice, so you'll need a way to show your face on camera (a small computer camera will be fine, or you could use a professional studio) and a way to input voice via a small computer microphone connected to your sound card.

Sometimes webinars include presentations using tools like PowerPoint or Web pages. In synchronous environments, visitors can browse the Web along with you. This is used most often for training environments where everyone is logged in and doing the training task while being taught. Sometimes webinars include file sharing and/or surveys and polls. We recommend requiring an email address before giving access to this information to help build your database of contacts.

You can accomplish a variety of goals with webinars. We recommend live educational seminars. You could, for instance, host a webinar on moving into a particular area and advertise it all over the Web. Those interested in moving into an area with which you're familiar can join; you get their contact information, and they get a great real estate professional to work with during their move.

If you decide to use this powerful tool, here are some things to think about. The number of registrants can be unlimited, and you should not charge for attendance. This tool is to make you the expert, the go-to person—you don't usually charge for that. If people perceive they are getting something for free, they're less leery of your intentions. Also, be sure you follow through afterwards. Collect email addresses. You may even have an "Opt In" box already checked to receive your newsletter; which you only send sparingly with relevant, important information Keep the length of the presentation manageable, both for you and for your audience. The time depends on the topic, but you don't want to put people to sleep (or yourself for that matter). The technology is only limited by your imagination.

Webcasts

You may choose to use webcasts instead of or as complements to webinars. *Webcast* is a generic term that refers to sending voice and video at the same time over the Internet. Webcasts predate podcasts. Believe it or not, this technology dates back to 1989! TV stations use them often; you can watch television shows you missed on the Internet. Today almost all major broadcasts have webcasts available on the Internet.

Companies Worth Noting

Remember to stay on top of who is playing the online real estate game and who's doing well at it. Knowing this will help you more successfully market yourself and partner with the organizations drawing the most attention, which will in turn help establish you as an expert.

In April 2005, REALTOR.com® had more than 2 million listings on its site, the largest audience of all online real estate companies to its business. This generated 6 million *different* visitors to the site. Note that some companies, when reporting their Web statistics, refer to "hits," or the number of times a page is requested. If the same person "hits" the page 20 times, that is 20 hits, which isn't an accurate representation of visitation. Also, the hits count is directly correlated with click-throughs (clicking through to another location or another site from your page), but the number of hits does not represent the exact number who will click through to other parts of your site or to other affiliate sites. Pay attention to these types of details when you go to partner with companies, and ask lots of questions. REALTOR.com® properly reported their information as *visitors*. Those numbers would make online companies in any industry envious. Stay tuned in to organizations that will begin competing directly with them, like Zillow.com.

The second most visited site is HomeGain.com, which had more than 3 million unique visitors in one month, again April of 2005. That same year, their six-month numbers were climbing 83 percent. HomeGain.com's research indicated that sellers who use the Internet

FIGURE 7.1 *Six-Month Growth of Top 10 Real Estate and Apartments Sites*

Site	April 2005 Unique Audience	November 2004 Unique Audience	Six-Month Growth
REALTOR.com	5,753,000	4,270,000	35 percent
HomeGain.com	3,133,000	2,356,000	33 percent
AOL Real Estate	2,670,000	855,000	212 percent
RealtyTrac	1,515,000	782,000	94 percent
Rent.com	1,366,000	733,000	86 percent
Yahoo! Real Estate	1,320,000	806,000	64 percent
Century 21	1,132,000	604,000	87 percent
forsalebyowner.com	990,000	409,000	142 percent
RealEstate.com	893,000	628,000	42 percent
RentNet	890,000	603,000	48 percent

Source: Nielsen/NetRatings, May 2005

to sell report higher sales prices than those using traditional means. In fact, for the months of June through August 2000, the average seller sold a home for over 15 percent more by using online methods over traditional ones. Companies like HomeGain.com also help consumers find an agent, especially one who claims to cater to the more educated and higher-income Internet buyer.

Although counterintuitive, it was reported in mid-2005 that lower-income households were the fastest-growing group of online real estate site visitors. According to Nielsen/NetRatings in May of 2005, Figure 7.1 represents the top sites and their unique visitors.

These numbers are astounding! The website *http:// allaboutmarketresearch.com* has a tremendous amount of information available on this topic, and you should spend some time with the numbers. The site reported:

Nielsen/NetRatings reported an overall jump in visitors from all income brackets to real estate and apartment sites during April 2005. Lower-income households earning up

FIGURE 7.2 *Household Income of Real Estate/Apartments Sites Visitors*

Household Income	April 2005 Unique Audience	Six-Month Growth
$0–$24,999	1,000,000	47 percent
$50,000–$74,999	6,179,000	32 percent
$150,000+	2,254,000	29 percent
$75,000–$99,999	3,983,000	24 percent
$100,000–$149,999	3,919,000	22 percent
$25,000–$49,999	3,966,000	20 percent

Source: Nielsen/NetRatings, May 2005

to $25K showed the most significant growth, with a million potential homebuyers and renters viewing a real estate or apartment site last month, marking a 47 percent leap during the past six months (see Figure 7.2).

This information is vital to your success. Let us move on to ways that you can use this information to help stake your claim as an expert in your area.

Incorporate the Web in Providing Outstanding Customer Service

One key to showcasing your area expertise online is by not only providing community information, links, and incorporating the best-of-breed applications into your site but also by providing outstanding customer service. One thing not often mentioned in real estate is the use of live chat. You see it at some sites these days—the ability to click "Get Live Help" or something similar on a website. Up pops a screen asking for your name and email address as well as your question. Why not offer this type of solution on your site? You can do so easily and inexpensively (even free!).

Our Web architect recommends this concept, and one method of achieving it is to use a tool like Live Help Messenger (*http:// livehelp.stardevelop.com*). You might have someone in your office respond to all of the requests when you aren't there to staff it. If you're worried about office hours or not being available 24/7, just note what times someone is available and give visitors an option to leave a message for you instead (and then get back to them right away). This way, potential clients or buyers can communicate their concerns to someone right away. You must answer every request in a timely manner, however, so be sure you have the staffing ready to support this. Perhaps even integrate live chat with your cell phone's text messaging capabilities so you can respond right away. This is a great tool with which to provide exemplary customer service and really shine against your competitors. Remember that dynamic websites really interact with you, even more so than podcasts and blogs. Incorporate as many elements of dynamic sites as you can into your Web interface.

Imagine how much more confident you'll feel about your business knowing that it is operating on the cutting edge of technology. Your clients will pick up on your confidence. They will appreciate how much time and effort you've invested in yourself and your business.

8 Create Lots of Repeat Business

TO MAINTAIN BUSINESS momentum, every real estate professional needs to create repeat business. Lots of professionals stay in
frequent contact with clients through the use of mailers, community brochures, fliers, postcards, and holiday cards. There are ways
to replicate this momentum online to generate repeat business.

Dynamic Newsletters and Interactive Tips—
Keep Your Customer Engaged

The use of online newsletters is Web 1.0 technology but still
fundamental for consistent success. Marketers talk about the five
to seven times it takes for someone to see or hear your name to
remember it and associate it with some particular facet of business. Providing a way for website visitors to sign up to be on your
monthly or quarterly mailing list is one easy way to stay in touch
with people and provide information in a push environment.

You can do this through a forum like Yahoo! Groups (Yahoo!
even provides the website code to add to your site), which keeps

people interested with links, files, and daily digest email. Then you can use the addresses in your list to send out repeat communications from your personal email account. You can also use lots of different Internet tools to create mailing lists and notify you each time someone asks to be put on the list. You can see an example of this at *http://commissions-at-risk.com* on the left-hand navigation bar. Cheryl Ann Henry, our Web architect/consultant, suggests holding contests online that encourage people to check back to see who won (much like "needing to be present to win," only online) as another way to keep people coming back. Perhaps sending an email reminder of the pending contest results and the winner announcements online would be useful. Actions like these can save the valuable time you used to spend going door to door in your neighborhood, introducing yourself and your services. As you know, many people are not receptive to sales calls at home. Email communication is much less intrusive.

Push versus Pull

Stepping back for a minute, we'll briefly discuss why using both the push and pull methods can be beneficial. In push marketing, you send data to someone; they are the recipient of your information. Some say this is "forced marketing," meaning that someone does not choose whether to receive it. It is important, therefore, to allow both for an opt-in and an opt-out method. While by law you have several days to remove people from your mailing list (the law varies by state), you will want to remove someone who wants out immediately. It only angers recipients if they are sent messages that they specifically asked not to receive. Again, we're only talking about email here, which someone can simply delete. This form of contact is less threatening than a phone call or knock on the door.

On the other hand, pull technology requires that the user or visitor actually request the information. For instance, if we go to

Zillow.com and request our current comparative analysis, we are "pulling" that information from the site; we choose to go there, and we go on our schedule. Ideally, you'll want to combine the freedom of choice (like pull technology) with good marketing (push technology) to keep people engaged and interested.

Be sure you time the emailed tips, newsletters, or whatever you decide to send. Make them newsworthy and timely and share your information or expertise. In other words, make them valuable to the recipient. One agent in our community sends out a quarterly flyer showing every home in the tract, including what it listed for, sold for, and its floor plan. While his method is a bit antiquated (I'd sure love to receive it by email), his information is relevant, timely, and interesting. It also keeps reminding the recipients of the agent's email address and phone number. You can do this in an online format; send out interesting and unique information that you, the community expert, know. You can usually be much more creative with online rather than paper-based communication. It is also much cheaper—think of the high printing and distribution costs you've had to pay in the past, not to mention the cost of mailing!

Meta Tags

Generating repeat business requires that you come up frequently in website searches. Be sure to use meta tags so that you are searchable and actually visit the "Add Site" features in search engines to list your site directly. A meta tag is like a small piece of information that is on the top of every Web page. It isn't necessarily visible but may be used only to define what your page is about. One meta tag is the title tag, which is literally the title of the page. But in addition to the title tag, two other tags make up meta tags: the meta description tag and the meta key words tag. (Actually, there is also a meta robots tag, but don't worry about that one.)

To give you an example, the title tag used at Microsoft's home page is "Microsoft Corporation." You can see how the title tag differs from the meta key words tag. The meta key words tag allows you to provide additional text that some crawlers of sites (that report back to search engines) use to index your site so the search engine can find it. Unfortunately, the meta key words tag has been so widely misused that now a lot of crawlers ignore it completely. It doesn't harm anything, but it may not do you any good, either. Examples of key words might be *real estate, mortgage,* and *home.*

Then there is the meta description tag. This does have an impact on how the crawlers see your site and how they report it to search engines. The crawler, a program that browses the Internet in a methodical but totally automated way, is what you need to rank your site. Usually up to 250 words can be indexed by a crawler. Some people just take the first two sentences or so of their Web page and use that as their meta description tag, but you should go further, in our opinions. Be very succinct and very clear. If you hired a Web developer, verify the quality of the meta description tag before the page goes live.

Emarketing versus Traditional Marketing

Remember that just because you embrace an emarketing campaign does not mean that you need to eliminate your traditional methods. You should use both, then carefully monitor which results in more listings, better service, and greater commissions. Emarketing can actually be better than traditional marketing. By using emarketing, you are creating a brand on the Internet. This is not easy to do using traditional means and is actually far easier using the dynamically built Internet. Internet marketing can allow for two-way communication channels, allowing you to create a community online. You are not certain who receives your hard-copy mailings or what people do with the information. With online communication, what people do with the information and what element is engaging are clearer. We have a lot of tools to help us assess communication's effectiveness, too. Rather than simply asking people, "Did you hear about us from our flyer?" you will know precisely when they got the email, how long before they clicked the link, what they did while they were there, and then how long before they phoned you. Be sure to ask your Web hosting company for the ability to collect these statistics.

Internet marketing has the element of immediacy, which can immediately impact your bottom line. Internet marketing creates a 24/7 environment, with information available for consumption at any time and feedback throughout the day. This also expands your market base to a global community, which isn't the case with traditional means. Also, people using the Web tend to have greater buying power; statistically speaking, they can afford the Internet, and they probably feel comfortable buying online. Responses can be analyzed in real time with minimal spending on advertising. One goal is obviously is to build your brand (and your brand may only be you), but also you want to attract new and old clients to your site.

Many experts advocate using podcasts to showcase success stories, get stories from clients, have them tell you in short "commercials" why they found your business model and your practice so attractive. Ask for their permission to put the video on your website and then use it to help build credibility. Unless your market is very specialized (e.g., luxury homes), it would be wise to get a wide cross-section of your clients that represents various socioeconomic backgrounds. This way, almost any potential client will be able to relate to your message.

All of this information is critical to generating repeat business. As a real estate professional, you want your name to be synonymous with high-quality work and area expertise. Your marketing campaigns can make or break that effort. Solicit the help of online newsletters (many are free of charge) and online mailing list management services and be sure to use a website hosting company that will give you vital statistics on click-thru rates and what pages are most visited on your site. Also, be prepared to make modifications to increase visibility.

Emarketing Quiz

HomeRoute™ (*www.homeroute.com*) publishes an "Emarketing Quiz" that answers the question "How Internet savvy are you?" It also offers other interesting tools on its site, including a blog and various topics for discussion. And it helps consumers find real estate professionals, so for that fact alone, it is worth a look! We thought it would be useful (and fun) to test yourself, so we've included the quiz below. As you take the quiz, write down your answers and then compare them against the answers and explanations found at the end of the quiz. Also, note any areas in which you feel you aren't quite up to speed.

Questions

1. Which items should be included in a marketing plan?
   (A) A brochure, a website, a newsletter, and ten mailings
   (B) A mailing list and a website domain name
   (C) A market analysis, goals, a budget, and a time line
   (D) A listings presentation that explains how you will advertise the seller's home

2. What generalizations can be made about a homebuyer who uses the Internet in his/her home search versus a traditional, non-Internet user?
   (A) Internet homebuyers tend to have lower credit scores.
   (B) Internet homebuyers often buy less expensive homes.
   (C) Internet homebuyers are generally less educated.
   (D) Internet homebuyers usually spend less time searching for a home.

3. An effective home page has which of the following characteristics?
   (A) Fast loading
   (B) Consistency
   (C) Clear and simple navigation

(D) Unique content

(E) All of the above

4. The best way to work with Internet-empowered consumers is to

(A) fax a buyer's agreement immediately.

(B) send a brochure by regular mail.

(C) work at their pace and patiently allow them to research on their own.

(D) keep exclusive control of property information and listings.

5. True or False: Once you develop a strong online marketing plan, you no longer need a strategy for offline marketing.

(A) True

(B) False

6. What percentage of homebuyers use the Internet in their search for a new home?

(A) 37 percent

(B) 65 percent

(C) 77 percent

(D) 95 percent

7. Which of the following examples of websites has the most effective combination of marketing elements?

(A) Descriptions of 25 homes for sale, 6 virtual home tours, and a "sneak preview" of weekend open houses

(B) A glamour photograph of you, a list of your designations and sales awards, and a comprehensive biography of you

(C) A look and feel that matches your print marketing materials with a personal message targeted towards a niche market and a "get more information" response form

(D) A list of hot links to 75 top real estate websites, a link to a website offering neighborhood crime and school reports, and a link to the public-access website of the local MLS

8. What should you include in your website design?
   (A) Your resume featured on your home page
   (B) A sampling of featured properties
   (C) Lots of pictures, sound bites, animation, and slide shows on your home page
   (D) Other than in your headline, 8-point text font

9. According to an Internet homebuyer, what is considered an acceptable amount of time for an agent to respond to an email message?
   (A) Some time the same day
   (B) By the next morning
   (C) Within 30 minutes
   (D) By the end of the week

10. This year, what percentage of their marketing budget are REALTORS® expecting to spend on online marketing?
    (A) 85 percent
    (B) 29 percent
    (C) 19 percent
    (D) 15 percent

11. What type of content will make your website more visible to search engines?
    (A) Creating page titles
    (B) Interlinking your pages back to your home page
    (C) Linking to other websites with related content
    (D) Unique community information
    (E) All of the above

12. Where are the best places to advertise your Web presence?
    (A) Mailings
    (B) Newsletters
    (C) Business cards

(D) Email signature

(E) All of the above

13. When selecting buyer's representation, how many agents do Internet homebuyers typically interview when making their choice?
    (A) 4
    (B) 3
    (C) 2
    (D) 1

14. To give users the right impression, which of the following suggestions is NOT a good idea when selecting a portrait or agent photo for your website?
    (A) Have a professional take it.
    (B) Use a recent digital picture.
    (C) Wear professional clothes, preferably dark colors.
    (D) Choose natural poses—avoid staged poses.

15. Which of the following describes an effective and captivating online home tour?
    (A) A sweeping panoramic scene of every level of the home
    (B) A video tour showing the seller's designer furniture, antique collectibles, and museum-quality artwork
    (C) A short, fast-loading preview that highlights the top features of a well-staged home
    (D) A 20-minute digital tour, including the neighborhood, the street, the exterior of the home, the neighboring homes, and every room in the house

16. What percentage of homebuyers work with the first real estate professional they talk to?
    (A) 48 percent
    (B) 65 percent
    (C) 76 percent
    (D) 99 percent

17. True or False: To increase your ability to capture leads on your website, visitors should have the ability to email you or contact you on EVERY page of your site?
   (A) True
   (B) False

18. Which of the following items should NOT be included in an email signature?
   (A) Your name with professional designations
   (B) Office/brokerage name
   (C) A list of recent awards and recognitions
   (D) Multiple phone numbers
   (E) Email address
   (F) Website address

19. When it comes time ultimately to buy a home, what percentage of Internet home researchers use a real estate agent?
   (A) 35 percent
   (B) 54 percent
   (C) 72 percent
   (D) 81 percent

20. When should you "give up" or discredit an online lead?
   (A) When they don't return your first call
   (B) One week after trying to contact them with no luck
   (C) One month after trying to contact them with no luck
   (D) Never

21. What is the average amount of time a visitor spends on a particular webpage before deciding whether to stay or leave?
   (A) 1 minute
   (B) 30 seconds
   (C) 15 seconds
   (D) 5 seconds

22. What are good resources to make available on your website?
    (A) Community information
    (B) List of local professionals (e.g., mortgage brokers, inspectors, etc.)
    (C) Local school reports
    (D) A sampling of current home listings
    (E) All of the above

Find the answers to the quiz questions on the following pages.

Answers

1. **(C) A market analysis, goals, a budget, and a timeline.**
   The items listed in the first two possible answers (brochures, websites, newsletters, mailings, and a domain name)
   are marketing tactics and tools. A listing presentation is an
   example of selling. Your marketing plan, on the other hand,
   should include details such as a market analysis, your goals,
   your budget, and a schedule.

2. **(D) Internet homebuyers usually spend less time searching for a home.** According to the California Association
   of REALTORS's® (C.A.R.) 2006 "Survey of Internet versus
   Traditional Home Buyers," the median age of Internet buyers was 39 years compared to a median age of 42 years for
   traditional buyers. Seventy-three percent of Internet buyers
   had at least a four-year college degree and an annual income
   of $184,900, compared with $148,910 for traditional buyers. Internet buyers spend on average only 2.2 weeks looking for the home they ultimately purchase, compared with
   7.1 weeks for traditional buyers.

3. **(E) All of the above.** It is important to remember that
   Internet users are generally impatient. If it takes longer than
   a few seconds for your site to load, they will leave. The home
   page should set the tone for the rest of the site's appearance. Consistency throughout the site makes the visitor feel
   more comfortable and be willing to complete an inquiry
   form. Also, how to navigate through your site should be
   clear. Buttons or links should appear on your home page
   to find secondary pages of your site. In addition, content
   is important on the home page to offer initial value and a
   reason to continue browsing your site. Most people don't
   appreciate a picture of the agent and another place to click
   before they see anything useful.

4. **(C) Work at their pace and patiently allow them to research on their own.** Respect the privacy of online consumers and allow them to decide when they are ready to make a commitment to buying a home with you. In the meantime, make it easy for them to find home listings on your website and let them know you are there to help them buy or sell a home when they're ready to take action. If you're too pushy, you'll scare them away. Demonstrating patience and taking time to cultivate a relationship will result in more success with online consumers.

5. **(B) False.** The goal of online marketing is to generate interest and create opportunities for you to connect with homebuyers and sellers in your local market. To impact your business, these connections need to move offline and develop into a working client relationship and, ultimately, a closed transaction. Real estate will always be a person-to-person business, and establishing marketing strategies to cultivate clients offline and build long-term loyalty is essential to securing long-term success in the industry.

6. **(C) 77 percent.** Last year, an estimated 77 percent of all U.S. homebuyers used the Internet in their search, according to the National Association of REALTORS'® (NAR) 2005 "Profile of Home Buyers and Sellers." This is an increase from 74 percent the year before. Ten years ago, only 2 percent of homebuyers used the Internet in their search.

7. **(C) A look and feel that matches your print marketing materials with a personal message targeted towards a niche market and a "get more information" response form.** The first choice (descriptions of homes, photo tours, and a "sneak preview" of open houses) is focused on property marketing and is missing an element of personal branding. The second choice (a glamour photograph, a list of your designations and sales awards, and a birth-to-present

biography) is too focused on you. And the fourth choice (links to 75 top real estate websites, links to neighborhood crime and school reports, and a link to the MLS website) consists solely of "exits" that direct consumers to other websites and away from your own.

8. **(B) A sampling of featured properties.** It is important to convey a professional image with your website. Although an important element in personalizing the consumer's experience, your "resume page" should be a secondary page that your prospect can choose to view. Font sizes smaller than 10 point will appear too small to read, especially on high-screen resolution. Remember, you have about ten seconds to capture a browser's attention, so don't add too many elements, like animation and sound, that will slow down the download process of your home page. Showcasing a few featured properties is a great way to capture your visitors' attention and motivate them to stay on your site longer!

9. **(C) Within 30 minutes.** Internet buyers expect a fast response from an agent. Of the buyers surveyed in C.A.R.'s "Internet versus Traditional Buyer" survey, 21 percent said they wanted an immediate response, and 23 percent wanted a response within 30 minutes. Non-Internet-using buyers are much more relaxed, with 38 percent being okay with a response from an agent at some point during the day, and 28 percent were fine with a response by the following morning.

10. **(B) 29 percent.** U.S. REALTORS'® anticipate spending more of their marketing dollars online this year and in the years ahead than in the past. As a result, they expect to spend less in print and elsewhere. This is according to a 2005 survey conducted by Classified Intelligence and Inman News Service. Compared to spending only 14 percent of their marketing budget online back in 2004, REALTORS'® self-

reported the online portion of their total marketing budget this year to jump to close to 30 percent, and they expect to spend even more in coming years.

11. **(E) All of the above.** Search engines are all the same in this way; they want to provide the most relevant results possible for their users. Unique content, navigation to relevant and related sites, and easy navigation and identification of what your site offers are all helpful in earning a higher ranking in the search engines.

12. **(E) All of the above.** Your domain name should be placed alongside your contact information in every type of print ad or electronic communication. When placing your website address in an email signature, be sure that it is linked directly to your site for easy navigation.

13. **(D) 1.** According to C.A.R.'s 2005 "Internet versus Traditional Buyers Survey," 71 percent of Internet users only interviewed a single agent, and that agent was the first to respond to their inquiry. A quick response may be the deciding factor in whether an agent wins the business of an Internet homebuyer. More and more consumers have high-speed Internet access, enabling them to gather information on all types of products and services quickly and easily. Internet homebuyers hold high expectations for an agent's response time.

14. **(B) Use a recent digital picture.** Digital pictures are not an acceptable replacement for a professionally taken portrait. Remember, you are the product. To set the right impression, be sure the portrait you choose represents a professional, authentic image—it is the first impression a potential client has of you.

15. **(C) A short, fast-loading preview that highlights the top features of a well-staged home.** The most effective

virtual tours move quickly and emphasize the home's scale, space, and proportions.

16. **(C) 76 percent of homebuyers work with the first real estate professional they talk to.** NAR's 2005 "Profile of Home Buyers and Sellers" revealed that 76 percent of homebuyers choose to work with the very first agent they talk to. Approximately half of the agents who responded to the 2006 "REALTORS® Technology Survey" indicated it takes them less than two hours to respond to a lead, and only 2 percent of the agents indicated that it took more than a day to respond. Real estate agents are coming to understand the need to respond quickly to online consumer inquiries.

17. **(A) True.** Clean and simple contact forms or a link to your email address should be accessible throughout your entire site. A consumer is more likely to leave your site rather than spending time looking for your contact information.

18. **(C) A list of recent awards and recognitions.** Information about your accomplishments is best reserved for an "About Me" section of your website. Your email signature is an extension of your business. It should be complete with accurate and multiple contact numbers and included in all online correspondence. Email signatures are often considered "virtual business cards" to today's online consumers.

19. **(D) 81 percent.** The Internet drives use of agents. According to NAR's 2005 "Profile of Home Buyers and Sellers," 81 percent of Internet searchers used a real estate agent in purchasing or selling a home, compared to 66 percent of non-Internet users.

20. **(D) Never.** Online consumers often behave very differently from traditional homebuyers. Findings from C.A.R.'s 2006 "Survey of Internet Buyers versus Traditional Buyers" found that Internet buyers spend approximately 5.8 weeks

researching their home purchase before contacting an agent for assistance, compared with only 2 weeks of research by traditional buyers. Therefore, a nonresponding online lead may simply be a consumer who is not yet ready to speak with an agent. However, this likely is still a legitimate prospective client. With Internet leads in particular, the importance of nurture marketing cannot be overstated. Placing nonresponding leads in an automated marketing campaign, whether it be a drip-email campaign, monthly newsletter mailing, or regular postcard mailings, that offers valuable resources early in the consumer's buying process will secure your position as the agent they think of first when they're ready to get serious and buy a home.

21. **(D) 5 seconds.** You have five seconds to place a compelling offer targeted at your site's visitors. Your landing page's headline is the first place most people will look, followed by any images or graphics. Be sure to choose the words and images on your site carefully.

22. **(E) All of the above.** Valuable, up-to-date resources and information are what consumers are looking for. Making your site the "one-stop resource" for your local area demonstrates value to a potential client. Remember, if you don't have the information on your site, the consumer will look somewhere else.

MySpace for My Real Estate Business?

We are often asked, "What role will MySpace have in my real estate business?" MySpace is the ultimately popular social networking site. Lots of businesses are creating profiles on MySpace, and there is an element of online self-definition based on who you choose to link to and list as a "friend." Recent media coverage has noted that many people are linking themselves to companies like Burger King or cell phone companies as statements about their personal preferences and tastes.

Should you also create a MySpace account? It can't hurt, particularly if you want to generate business with the Gen-Xers and Gen-Yers who are frequent visitors to these sites. Remember that these generations aren't just first- or second-time homebuyers; they are also investors who are turning to real estate rather than the stock market for stable investments. What you will need to determine is whether you want to use a personal profile or a business one—if you want to list information about *you* so people can get to know you and feel comfortable with you, or if you'd prefer to create a company profile to give a little personal insight but a lot of professional data. The personal sites do better with an audience like the one at MySpace, but not everyone is comfortable mixing their personal and professional lives. The choice is really up to you but do consider MySpace as a potential marketing medium for your business.

Check out the following MySpace page: *http://groups.myspace.com/MLSonMySpace*. It is geared towards helping real estate professionals promote their businesses online. It currently has a growing list of about a thousand members. How do you see yourself using MySpace to create an online personality? It may or may not fit your business goals, but it should be considered.

9 Maintain Momentum in Any Market Condition

MARKET CONDITIONS ARE constantly shifting, and technology is playing a role in the change. We saw an incredible real estate boom fueled by speculators and low interest rates. Then a couple of years later, an interest rate hike coupled with excess inventory created a depressed market in some areas. Speculation and low unemployment helped some markets rebound well. While homeowners and investors are concerned with and even troubled by changing market conditions, the real estate professional is quite vulnerable to them. While it is impossible to recession-proof your business, it is possible to create such a strong sense of loyalty to you and your work that you will be the go-to person regardless of the market condition. You can use technology to help build this loyalty.

Stay Ahead of Technology—The Zillow Effect!

The next logical question of course is "How?" One way is to stay on top of the real estate marketplace and how technology is changing it. New products are being released monthly that can help you maintain your momentum in spite of down markets. Stay on top of the latest and greatest information and know your competition.

For instance, in December 2006, Zillow.com announced its entry into the real-estate-for-sale listings market. According to *Real Estate Industry Tech News* (a blog source that we check at least weekly at *www.realestateblogsites.com/public/blog/144934*), Zillow.com is directly challenging the MLS system that's been in place for 100 years. Many real estate professionals (and lots of consumers) dislike the current MLS system. Also, market downturns often require extreme marketing measures, and using this tool is one of many ways to help increase listing hits. All on one map, a potential homebuyer can search for homes (with overlays of landmarks, water, roads, etc.) for homes for sale, homes just sold, and homes with "make me move" prices. Clicking on a home gives the estimated comparative analysis and just about any bit of demographic data you could want as a buyer. As a real estate professional, you need to review Zillow.com's tools for real estate professionals and be intimately familiar with what your clients are seeing. Integrated with mapping tools, demographic tools, and satellite imagery, the site is a powerful marketing force.

Inman News reported ten reasons that Zillow.com's move is significant to the real estate industry:

1. Zillow.com is an alternative to the 100-year-old MLS system. It is building its own database and can do whatever it likes with the data.

2. It is a centralized real estate information and communication hub.

3. The site offers an incredible mix of user tools, including a great user interface, innovative maps, and wiki user editing features. It brings "some of the best thinking around Web 2.0 applications to tap into the real estate obsession" (Inman News 2006).

4. It is relying on user-generated content in a new but familiar way for real estate professionals. Zillow.com lets homeowners list their own homes! This is something they previously have not been able to do easily.

5. Zillow.com gets listings from agents and consumers; this may allow the company to sidestep copyright claims and industry constraints. Other companies have gone the "permission-content" route, asking MLS organizations or brokers for permission to display listings. The Zillow model does not look as though it will have those constraints.

6. Property record data and listing data are all mixed dynamically. The property record database establishes baselines for listings, which will help price them more accurately.

7. A need for great timing in a slowing market has agents trying to get more exposure for listings to help impatient sellers. Because Zillow.com is free, agents have no obvious reason not to use it. Consumers will also like the no-cost structure.

8. It is the first online company to experiment seriously with direct home-selling models, including allowing sellers to entertain offers directly from prospective buyers.

9. The industry action will be intense, possibly involving the Justice Department and the Federal Trade Commission (is any publicity bad?).

10. This is only the beginning. As more capital is provided for online real estate ventures, investors and entrepreneurs will follow Zillow.com's lead.

By the time this book goes to print, you will probably be well aware of the release and the product. But were you aware of it on the day the company made the announcement? You can stay on top of this type of information by subscribing to forums and blogs and by talking with other professionals, attending seminars, and reading books. Staying on top of insider industry news is important to maintaining your momentum in any market. Another way to do it is through the same technology you will use to reach your Web-savvy clients, including RSS feeds and newsgroup subscriptions. Subscribe to those with tech tip forums and network with others who have similar goals.

What else is your competition doing? Well, for starters, they are offering online listings, and they are offering *flat fees* and *unbundling of services,* which we advocate. Have you seen the following sites? They are all using distinctive models, and they may all directly compete with the way you do business:

- ListByOwnerOnMLS.com, a subsidiary of BrokerDirect-MLS.com (*www.listbyowneronmls.com*)
- ADDVantage™ Real Estate Service (*http://getmoreoffers.com*)
- FlatFeeListing™ (*http://flatfeelisting.com*)
- For Sale By Owner.com (*www.forsalebyowner.com*)

Remember, many sellers are enamored with the incredible amount of money they can get for their home these days. A home that was worth only $500,000 a few years ago may now be pushing $800,000 or $900,000, and to that owner, $54,000 in commissions at 6 percent, regardless of how justifiable by the profession, isn't an option. We realize many of you frequently sell homes for 4.5 to 5 percent, but even that reduced fee doesn't compete with the 2–3 percent that flat-fee and low-cost brokers offer or those homeowners who are selling by owner can pay. With buyers knocking on the door, they have less reason than ever to use a professional agent to sell their home. The real estate spike has created tremendous equity for a lot of people—a lot of potential sellers who frankly don't want to pay what they consider a lot of money to sell their home professionally. Discount and flat-fee brokers are popping up everywhere as a result of technological advances and homeowners' desire to keep more money in their own pockets.

Current home prices have ventured outside the realm of affordability for many home seekers, because their rate of appreciation in recent years has far outpaced that of earnings. For real estate agents, however, commissions are based on a percentage of home prices. Therefore, the higher the price, the greater the commission. If a home doubles in value over a few years (which many homes did during the recent boom), a real estate agent can earn double the commission than just a few years before. How many other professions enjoyed this same increase in compensation for their workers? Many home sellers now question whether the hefty commissions were warranted. After all, the same agents were earning a fraction of this amount for the same work only a few years before.

Flat-Fee Companies and the Internet

Some flat-fee companies charge under $500 to list homes in the MLS. Often, the seller who uses these systems still has to pay a 2–3 percent to the buyer's agent, but that is far less than the standard 5–8 percent, particularly on an expensive home sale. Arising from this has been a "war" between traditional real estate professionals and those who help people market their homes for sale by owner. The professionals' traditional commission structure will be changed drastically by companies that discount, by Internet-based organizations, and perhaps even by the government and regulation. REAL *Trends* consistently reports record-breaking real estate commissions, and these new heights are tied directly not only to low interest rates, which increase demand, but also to the high price of homes.

The most important role that discounters play in the sale is to put the home up in the MLS database. There are more than 1,000 MLSs in the United States, and as you well know, these databases are local-market driven. While discounters may skimp on service and don't always get the highest price for the seller, people are often willing to take that chance to save a lot of money. As the Web becomes more prominent and companies provide more services online, you can expect this trend to continue.

Begin thinking of how you'll compete directly with this type of organization, because your future will depend on it. Rather than fighting technological advancement, consider embracing it yourself. Don't count on states to pass minimum service laws (laws that prohibit brokers from listing homes on the MLS without also providing basic services, like contract negotiation and receiving offers). Remember that the Federal Trade Commission and the Justice Department have not been happy with these rules, and we've yet to see how they will play out in the long term.

One thing that these online organizations do well is provide a *self-service list of dos and don'ts for sellers.* For instance, many offer blogs or podcasts with information on eliminating smells, cleaning up your home, and holding open houses. This is your competition, whether you believe it yet or not; so you need to incorporate this type of information into your own dynamic site. You may even consider a more extreme measure—unbundling your services, explaining each service on your site, and letting your clients choose the ones that they want. This is essentially an á la carte model that lets individuals decide what is needed and lets them add additional services later if their property isn't moving quickly enough.

Pay attention to full-service companies like ZipRealty that also offer cheaper prices. Based in Emeryville, California, this company usually gives sellers 1 percent off of the standard market commission rate in their area and often gives buyers a 20 percent rebate on commissions. The organization employs over 1,500 agents. Some even offer frequent flyer miles or gift cards to stores like Home Depot. Whatever you decide to offer and however you decide you can best compete, document your services and strategies well on your site. Know who your FSBO competitors are, too, including MLS4owners.com (*http://mls4owners.com*), Property Pig™ (*http://propertypig.com*), Assist-2-Sell (*http://assist2sell.com*), For

Sale By Owner.com (*www.forsalebyowner.com*), Redfin (*http://redfin.com*), and Help-U-Sell® Real Estate (*http://helpusell.com*) among many others.

Finally, pay attention to sites that are dedicated to *fee transparency*. Yes, these sites do exist. Check out Lowerfees (*http://lowerfees.com*). This site will actually break down notary fees, title fees, broker or agent fees, document fees, postage and courier fees, wire transfer fees—you name it—all based on property type and location. It is designed to help individuals negotiate fees and understand what is reasonable and what is not. A quick search of one author's home price and zip code revealed precisely what should be paid and for what service—and even recommended providers who will stay within that range. Consider offering your services to this organization! To give you an example, it indicated that the total fees for one transaction should be about $5,870.00. Is that what you would have calculated for a $1 million home? We're guessing not. Understand this system and its role in real estate.

Using the Internet to Build Business in Down Times

Let us talk about additional Internet technologies that will help you thrive in any market condition. Many experts agree that one way for real estate professionals to grow in any market is to offer online services, not just marketing information. Still, a combined approach of traditional and Internet marketing is required to get clients to your site so they can begin to use your online services. One way to do this is to know what visitors to your site come there for, so you can make sure you're providing it easily and quickly. One free tool do to this is called Google Analytics. You can view the tool and its product information at *www.google.com/analytics/*. The tool can provide you with more than 500 different statistics to help you learn more about your site's visitors and their behavior. The software analyzes information that is stored in a log file on a website and provides charts and graphs to help you understand your business better—and, more importantly perhaps, what happens when a website visitor goes to your site.

What about these services that keep people coming back to, and staying at, your website? Try offering links to Neighboroo (*http://neighboroo.com*) when your potential prospects click on homes you have for sale. This relatively new site provides household income information, tax rates, unemployment data, population density, apartment rents, air quality, elementary school rankings, and even political information, all at the users' fingertips. Remember, you don't have to reinvent the wheel to provide great services, just be sure to embrace the new technological advances as they hit your market. You want your clients accessing this information, and even finding out about it, through you—not another agent.

Another great tool is a direct competitor to Zillow.com: eppraisal.com (*http://eppraisal.com*). Eppraisal.com provides instant computerized appraisal information to any consumer. If you're suggesting a homeowner list their home at $300,000, for instance, and they find out on eppraisal.com that some estimate their home is worth $340,000, they may assume you were trying to "keep the data from them." In fact, this information may not necessarily be reflecting the current market but instead previously closed listings, and may be taking into account other factors, like view lots, that consumers may not realize. One way to combat such misunderstandings is to put a link on your website, then discuss the information with the client—full disclosure. Let them know what other homes have sold for and then why you are suggesting pricing their home as you are.

Multifamily Residential

Gaining momentum in any market condition isn't limited to the residential real estate sector. The multifamily housing arena relies on renting out apartments, homes, and multifamily units for revenue and survival. While we intend to write an entire book on this topic (multifamily markets have their own special requirements and interests), a few lessons from successful multifamily companies and businesses are easily applied to both the residential and multifamily arenas. The concept of being consumer driven is applied in the multifamily area as being resident driven. Take a look at the products offered by 365 Connect (*http://about365.com*). In the multifamily arena, it is precisely the type of technology that will help manage your existing business and grow your market for the future. One key to dynamic websites is that their information changes based on visitor selection and criteria—precisely what this system does. The resident portal lets the site owner provide technically savvy community tools to help visitors stay engaged and to retain them as clients. While letting property managers more efficiently manage their business, it simultaneously offers residents technology that lets them stay connected.

Bring the Services Together—Keep People on Your Site

With any system, regardless of your market (multifamily or residential), one main goal of your website is to help bring all of your services together into one place so that you can keep people on your page longer. Therefore, you want your solution providers to be not only an extension of your business, but also to integrate seamlessly with your Web presence—a fine line that is sometimes difficult to walk. For example, the 365 Connect system lets residents submit service requests online, pay rent, reserve amenities, turn on utilities, and get lots of local information. From your professional perspective, it saves time by autodialing people if they are late with rent; allowing you to see what's going on in your community in real time; and offering email, Web hosting, File Transfer Protocol (FTP) services—you name it. Many sites offer such services that try to keep individuals on the site so that the business can capture the audience and the market. This strategy, always a good idea, is part of exceptional marketing.

One critical characteristic of today's online real estate consumers is that they tend to move around frequently and they tend to make big moves more often than many realize. Sometimes moves are for job or family reasons, sometimes for a change of pace. Whatever solution you implement, you'll want to make sure that they can easily find your website before their move, because this is often when decisions are made about neighborhoods, if not specific communities. Your residential site needs to contain information on the neighborhood, demographics, maps, tools to everything imaginable (restaurants, gas stations, etc.), and perhaps even overlays of the closest parks and rivers. So does your apartment portal if you are in the multifamily business (yet another great reason to check out 365 Connect). While many real estate professionals still believe that "real estate is a local business," it is becoming more national and even global today than ever, and we don't see this trend changing.

In an electronic interview with Kerry W. Kirby, president and CEO of 365 Connect, we asked him several questions about hosting the residential website and many technology questions associated with blogs, podcasts, and Web hosting. His answers provide some insightful information into the way that technology companies are using the Internet to enhance the real estate business.

Q: *Do you integrate podcasting and blogs in your software? Do you see them playing a role in this market space in the future? What if someone already has one set up?*

A: We design and host websites. Our products are marketing sites (e.g., *http://whiterockapts.com*) and a very robust resident service portal (150 pages deep). The concept is to bring an apartment community's leasing and management operation fully online. [Note from authors: This is a critical element in multi and residential markets.] In short, anything you can do by walking into the management office, we enable online.

A blog is only as good as its blogger. We have set up forums for residents (once they are a resident) inside the portal. If you ever walk through a sizable apartment community, you will find flyers, usually by the mail kiosk (e.g., I want to sell my sofa, I lost my cat, etc.). This interaction will take place among residents no matter what, so we brought that piece online. [Note from authors: Yet another important element! All of the things you sit down with and discuss with potential clients should be on your website.]

Managers are fearful of this, as they all flock to *www. apartmentratings.com* to see the bad things residents write about their community, so they think this is the same. We enabled a system for "Residents Only" to post on; we made the residents the "police" of the forums with a "Report This Posting" link. A manager can also look up with a single click who posted what—and they have an option to edit or delete it. In our business, we have to serve two masters, resident and manager.

We think as content feeds evolve, this will evolve into a valuable tool at the resident level and we will use it as the demand grows. We are also looking into video; it is BIG!

All that being said, we are working on an "Industry" website that we plan to launch called Multifamily-Biz.com. Our idea is to enable people in the industry to run blogs, podcast, provide news content from their individual market areas, and even hold webinars on their products and services. [Note from authors: Again, very valuable in the real estate single and multifamily markets.] We see no true "hub" in the multifamily industry for people to obtain resources from. As large as this industry is (Harvard released info this year that rental housing provides housing for over 34 million people, and there is currently $2.7 trillion in rental stock) there is no single source where a vendor, owner, developer, etc., can go to obtain information. In New Orleans, the cost of insurance is killing multifamily developments; I would love to read the postings of a blogger from New Orleans on this issue. This is a project we are doing on our own; we want to help in educating this industry and provide a platform for people to interact with their peers. [Note from authors: One of your jobs as single family agents and multifamily professionals is to educate your consumer base. Often education is the main competitive advantage that a real estate agent has over a Web-based system—the ability to explain a complicated industry to people who don't often transact.]

Q: *How is your site dynamic as opposed to Web v1?*

A: We believe a common thread is weaving the Web into the new marketplace: integration. 365 Connect has been a hub for integration with the best of breed service providers in the multifamily industry. [Note from authors: There are top companies we discuss doing this in residential as well.] We have built integrations with renters' insurance companies, where a resident obtains real-time pricing and purchases a policy inside our portal in minutes; the same goes for rent payments, utility transactions, etc. Through Web services, we can keep a resident inside our secure encrypted environment and transmit data back and forth in real time server to server. The evolution of the Web is to work with others, deliver their services to your clients (residents), and not try to be everything to everybody. Embrace what others have created; use it to enhance your Web products. This is what Amazon.com has done to grow beyond a bookstore. [Note from authors: This integration is what we advocate throughout this book for your own website. The more information, links, and resources you can offer from best-of-breed companies—even those you may see as competitive forces like Zillow.com—the more you will embrace technology, and the more your client base will see you as a leader.]

Q: *Anything else you'd add about the business model and technology solutions that you feel is important?*

A: My team is made up of what I call a crazy mix. I have almost become a hub for computer science seniors from a local university. I am a multifamily developer by trade and saw the evolution of how residents were coming to properties we were building via the Internet. I was an early adopter of using websites for my business. By the time we stepped into the early 2000 era, we saw 20 Internet inquiries to 1 phone call. We then said, "We need to serve this market."

I think our team mix brings a different perspective to what we are doing. I know the business from the ground up; I know manager, resident issues, etc. My tech team is Gen-Y, so they know what their generation wants on the Web and how to execute it. [Note from authors: This is absolutely critical! As noted in both *Commissions at Risk* and this book, what the younger Gen-Xers and the Gen-Yers want from you are entirely different than what previous generations want.] They are the "MySpace" generation, and the creation of community on the net is very important to them. They see what we are doing as a mission to deliver this platform to their generation. They cannot believe the multifamily industry ignores their "techiness." To them, what we're doing makes so much sense.

Gen-X and Gen-Y are our new renters. Combined, this group is 107 million strong in America. Our model is simple: Bring the leasing and management operation online, because these are our new renters and this is how they like to do business. Wake up and cater to the new market! What did Sears do when their business was dying?

Q: *What are you doing to help your clients be more efficient and better at their business?*

A: We are always doing new things to take more of the task away from them. Like we (on the 365 Connect side) now load a new community newsletter every month, and they can add to it if they wish (99 percent don't). Our entire service costs less than a paper newsletter service by the way. We are also launching a new way for residents to gain access to the portal, as the managers don't seem to put them in (it takes 28 seconds—we timed it). We saw this need when we started getting emails from residents asking how they could gain access (we remain seamless, so it took some effort for a resident to find us). If that is not demand for Web-based services, what is?

The multifamily industry has a hard time seeing value, unless it equates to money in their hand. So we will now launch a system early next year where a community can partner with local retailers and turn our Web products into ancillary income by selling them ad space in the portal (captive audience). [Note from authors: We discuss this method later in our book.] Our research shows that retailers (from the dry cleaner to the pizza place) come to multifamily properties all the time wanting to put flyers out. We have a community counting for us, and they have averaged 17 requests a month. According to our math, it cost more to post, say, 300 flyers only to create trash for the service crew to pick up than pay, say, $50 a month for a graphic, a description of services, and a link. Again, according to the latest propaganda, Gen-X and Gen-Y are looking for you online.

10 Final Thoughts

REAL ESTATE IS a constantly evolving business. Sometimes it is difficult to determine which technologies you should embrace. Real estate professionals are always busy and often don't have time to understand the technology, or we are too stubborn to let go of traditional methods that we've used throughout our careers. Yet even if you devote only 15 minutes per day to understanding the online technology that we've described in this book, you'll understand much more about the industry's inevitable future.

Agents spend a great deal of time generating lists of the advantages they provide and the reasons they will never be without work. Most seem to dismiss market evolutions that have already taken place in the travel and financial industries. However, there will be a day when a real estate agent simply does not exist without technology—or a day where individuals can buy and sell homes directly without involving an agent at all. We know as technologists that the day will come. As a real estate professional, you have a choice to make: continue to do business the way you have and retain a small segment of the market, or be part of the revolutionary changes in real estate taking place online.

Don't make assumptions about what the public knows. The average buyer or seller may avoid representation unless they know why agents are important. Those who list with an agent are doing so because they feel you know more about the process than they can learn on their own on the Web—that is the essence of the transparency we see in the marketplace today. Describe yourself and your expertise so people feel a need to work with you. Technology increases transparency, but it also increases accountability; covering up your pricing strategy and your commissions rate will not work in this information-hungry environment. We encourage you to hire a Web architect soon to embrace the concept of Web services, not just Web marketing. In fact, we strongly believe your long-term livelihood depends on it.

It is not our intention to belittle the services that real estate agents currently provide. In fact, we firmly believe that the recent surge in home prices was due in large part to the expertise that real estate agents provided and the value that they added. Having said that, however, we all have to realize that the times they are a-changin'. None of us can change or ignore this powerful trend. Our point of view is that there is no reason to try to ignore it. We believe that a moderate modification in the way you do business is all you need to adapt and, ultimately, not only survive but also flourish.

Frequently Asked Questions (FAQs)

Every good website has an FAQ section—yours should, too! An FAQ section is often the first link visitors follow to find key information about a website's creators, origins, and purpose. Perhaps you have similar questions for us that we can answer in our own FAQ, which you'll find below, just after a list of our top ten tips for podcasts and blogs.

Tips for Podcasts and Blogs

1. *Update your podcasts often.* If you want people to keep coming back, your content has to remain original. If you're using a podcast to showcase your current listings, this is especially important.

2. *Be consistent.* Pretty soon, you'll have an entire series of podcasts and blogs. You should have a consistent theme throughout with regard to the look and feel. This will serve as your own trademark.

3. *Be both timely and timeless.* Your content has to be timely in terms of the issues that are most appealing to people at that particular time (e.g., current interest rates), but at least a portion of it should not be time-specific so it does not become stale in the near future.

4. *Sacrifice some speed for quality.* In our opinion, it is preferable to have a presentation-quality podcast that takes a while to load than to have a low-quality one that loads right away. The initial extra wait is well worth it.

5. *Preparation is key, but scripting is not.* When recording your podcast, you certainly need to be prepared for the content that you'll be providing. However, don't script it or you risk sounding stiff and impersonal.

6. *Conduct interviews.* Don't assume that you know exactly what people are going to want to see in your blogs and podcasts. Why go through the trouble of creating content only to have to revise it significantly later? Find out up front and minimize the rework.

7. *Don't take personal attacks personally.* Not everyone subscribes to the addage "If you don't have anything nice to say, don't say anything at all." If you do receive some negative feedback on your blog or podcast, look at it constructively and definitely don't allow it to discourage you in any way.

8. *Get your own domain name if you don't already have one.* Although there are plenty of ready-made platforms out there for blogs and podcasts, using one is impersonal and makes you appear as one in a sea of many. Therefore, make a small investment at the outset to secure your own domain name. In time, it will come to be closely associated with you.

9. *Come up with a hooking strategy.* Very often, attracting new users and hooking users require two different strategies. Ask yourself the following two questions, and hopefully some aspects of each answer will be different: (1) What do I need to do to get people to visit my blog and/or view my podcast? (2) What do I need to do to create enough interest to have people keep returning to my blog and viewing my podcast?

10. *Comment on other blogs.* A great way to spread the word about your own blog is to post on other people's blogs, especially if those blogs are popular. Make sure your posts are interesting enough to generate interest in your own blog, but definitely don't simply advertise your blog without adding value.

Frequently Asked Questions

1. *Do I need to buy an iPod to create a podcast?* You don't know the answer to this by now? :) You absolutely and most certainly *do not* need an iPod.

2. *Okay, so if I don't need an iPod, then why do they call it "podcasting?"* Well, the name actually does originate from the word *iPod*. It's basically a combination of *iPod* and *broadcasting*. We wish that we had enough influence to change the name, because it is confusing!

3. *How large can my podcast be?* As large as you want, but keep in mind that the larger it is, the more time it takes to

download. Therefore, people with slower connections may be turned off.

4. *How do I know if my podcast is successful?* First, you'll have to define what success means to you. If it's a certain number of downloads, a third-party hosting service can provide these numbers for you. However, if it's your bottom line, then it's up to you to determine how much your business has increased as a result.

5. *Can I legally add copyrighted music to my podcast?* In short, no. Many people do without realizing that it's illegal. However, many up-and-coming musicians are willing to provide podsafe music.

6. *Is it expensive to create a blog? Expensive* is a relative term, but the answer is probably no by most people's definition. In fact, Blogger allows you to do it for free.

7. *How do I advertise my blog?* Of course, you can use methods like emailing and your existing advertising, However, we believe that the actual content will go a long way towards spreading the word.

8. *What should I include in my blog?* Look at other blogs for ideas but certainly don't copy them. A great way to start is to interview your existing clients!

9. *Are there directories of blogs to which I can add my blog?* Absolutely. Check out Bloghub and Bloggeries. There are many others as well.

10. *What is RSS?* It stands for Rich Site Summary (Web version 1) or Really Simple Syndication (Web version 2). It's basically a way for blog sites to share headlines much the way syndication works in newspapers.

Logging Off

Technology is not a cyclical fashion or flavor of the day; it is a perpetual evolution that has affected every aspect of our lives. Real estate is no exception. In fact, real estate is primed for such a progression because of the high number of manual processes that are incorporated into even the most basic transactions.

You bought this book because you were either interested in technology or afraid of it. If you were one of those people who knew just enough about technology to feel intimidated by it, then this book has hopefully expanded your horizons and helped you to understand better how to implement what's out there. It is not our intent to make anyone feel threatened or concerned by technology—quite the contrary. No matter how many new sites come onto the scene, we believe that the world needs real estate professionals. Without them, the recent housing boom might have never existed, home values would have remained stagnant, and the market stability that we take for granted couldn't occur. No doubt your clients would risk lots of legal problems without your professional guidance.

We also believe, however, that real estate pros need to rethink the way that they do business to stay competitive in the future. As technologists, we perceive the changing marketplace in a way that those close to the day-to-day work of real estate may not. We recommend that you take the time to visit every site mentioned in this book and make sure that you grasp the concept of the site, what message it is trying to send, and how successfully it sends it. We have made it our careers to share our impressions and expectations with you. We hope you will decide to embrace our advice and enjoy a flourishing and exciting new marketplace.

Finally, we would love to hear from you. If you decide that you're going to stick with the traditional path to acquiring and maintaining clients, then we want to know why. If you decide, as we have, that there's no fighting the future marriage of technology and real estate services, then we want to know why. Many of you may fall somewhere in between; that is, you respect technology, but you do not feel that it is necessarily going to make or break you. Or you might implement a nice cookie-cutter website that you will use to allow others to get to know about you and your services—and nothing more. We hope you won't be satisfied with mediocrity! However, whichever path you decide to take, we wish you the best of luck and a bright future.

A Terms and Definitions

IF YOU ARE interested in expanding on any of these terms and definitions, we recommend that you type in the word along with *definition* into Google. Several great resources can help you explore each of these definitions more fully and give you a deeper understanding of how to implement the various products and technologies. Some can't-miss sites are HowStuffWorks (*www.howstuffworks. com*), Whatis?com (*http://whatis.techtarget.com*), and Wikipedia (*http://wikipedia.org*).

Adobe Flash Adobe Flash is an Adobe Systems product that is often used in website development. Flash has an authoring application as well. It is one of the most common applications used in websites. It is used to add graphics and animated activity to Web pages.

Atom Atom is a pair of standards. Atom Syndication Format is XML that is used for Web feeds. Atom Publishing Protocol is a very simple set of rules (language) used for Web resources.

A Web feed can be downloaded by websites or by users that subscribe to a feed to view its content.

Blog A blog is a user-generated website often referred to in Web 2.0. Notations or entries are created in what looks like an online journal or note pad. They are often embedded within Web pages to create a community or forum. A blog often has numerous components, including text, links, other Web pages, graphics, and notes and news. Blogs can be used in real estate to create a community or network where people come to read your latest news and writing, usually in an interactive format.

Blogcast A blogcast is the combination of a blog and a podcast on one website. The site can be found by search engines, making the podcast searchable.

Blogger This is someone who has his/her own blog. A blogger can be anyone; the blogger need not be a professional who blogs for a living nor a member of the media.

Blogosphere The blogosphere is all blogs out there on the Internet as a community. The interactive and community nature of blogs means that many bloggers link to one another, which creates a big interconnected network of blogs. You will want to be sure to post on others' blogs as well as your own. By becoming a member of the blogosphere, you will increase name recognition, and you will attract others to your blog, too. Be sure you link other blogs to yours and offer enough content that they want to do the same!

Domain Name A domain name is the name that you type into a Web browser to get to a website. For instance, if you type in *kaplan.com,* you will go to Kaplan's website. The domain name is important, because your business is often known by its name. Sometimes people choose to buy domain names that are not synonymous with or the same as as their business's name. For example, you might work for a real estate broker who owns a company called Great Real Estate, but you may choose to have a domain name like *www.youshouldbuymyrealestate.com*. You might pick a different name for marketing purposes. You might also have two names, one which directs visitors to the other site. This is known as URL forwarding. You can also GRIP a URL, which means that if you are hosting your site on your own Internet space through your Internet service provider, you can still use *youshouldbuymyrealestate.com* and have your service provider show only that domain name (not the actual, often convoluted name) in the Web browser. These powerful tools will help you maintain the integrity and consistency of your site.

Dynamic Web Page Dynamic Web pages are pages that are not static; that is, they change based on the user, the user's preferences, or the instructions on the user's computer. This creates interactivity that standard Web pages do not provide. Our Web architect, Cheryl Ann Henry, recommended we all build dynamic sites. The dynamic features allow the user to feel as though the site was custom-designed just for him/her and encourage the user to come back often.

Electronic Commerce (Ecommerce) Ecommerce is the Internet marketplace. Any site that is used to sell or buy products or services is an ecommerce site. For instance, Amazon.com and eBay are ecommerce sites. Even if you are only using your site to provide information on your services, it would still be considered an ecommerce site.

HTML HTML is HyperText Markup Language. It is the most commonly used language on the Internet. If you go to your Web browser and go to "View" and then "Source," you can see the HTML code that is used to generate the page you are viewing. HTML code is what programmers write to make your Web page accessible and viewable by a Web browser.

HTTP Hypertext Transfer Protocol (HTTP) transfers information on the Internet onto your computer screen when you are surfing the Web. It facilitates requests by the user or server, then responds to the user or server. HTTP, although unseen, is required to make the Web work. When you look in your Web browser, before the domain name is the *http://* notation. This indicates to the Web browser that the protocol it should be communicating with is Hypertext Transfer Protocol and not another that your browser supports, like File Transfer Protocol (FTP). On the other hand, if you decide to design your own site from a template and you upload information, you will type *ftp://* into your Web browser or into an FTP utility.

Home Page The home page is the URL that is loaded automatically when you go to a page. For example, if you type in *www.google. com,* you may really be taken to *www.google.com/index.html.* Although you will be unaware of this, technically the *index. html* file is the home page. When you click "Home" on the site, the site takes you to the home page. You want your home page to be inviting and encouraging to visitors. Sites are usually known by their home page, so this is a critical element that sets the tone for your work and your visitors' expectations.

iPod iPod was created and launched by Apple in 2001. iPods have become a bit of a phenomenon and, some say, have restored Apple's success in the marketplace. Apple's iPod uses iTune software to communicate. A common misunderstanding is that you must have an iPod to listen to a podcast. In fact, you can download Apple's iShare software from *www.apple.com* without having an iPod. Some iPod models let you watch video, read books, and listen to audio. The iPod has spun off numerous other technologies from Apple and other companies.

Internet The *Internet* is the term encompassing the entire network of all computers that make up not only the Web but email, File Transfer Protocol, and all of the other sites and computers on the public network. The Internet is a network of networks that was originated by universities and the government. Today, it is used for everything from email to chat to phone calls. What we commonly call the *Internet* is really the Web; that is, anything you see in a Web browser on your PC, your handheld device, etc.

Meta Tags Meta elements are important in your website, because they define the data about your website's contents and identify how your site will be retrieved in search engines. Search engines will crawl your site for these meta tags, using the meta tags as the search criteria. Make sure your Web designer knows the essential key words you want used for the site and includes them. It is easier to include them at the beginning of the site development rather than going back and adding them later. Adding them later can cause confusing and conflicting information in search engines, and because the engines have already crawled your site, they may not go back to look for updates. However, you can force search engines to look for updates or use specific key words through tools available on each of the search engine sites and through third-party applications.

Moblog Moblog is a combination of a Web blog and mobility applications (such as cell phones). The moblog first emerged in Japan, where camera phones were of high quality and had a lot of bandwidth.

MySpace.com MySpace is a social networking website offering an interactive environment that relies on relationships. Individuals create their site (so do products and businesses by the way!), and users who want to be identified by their "friends" add those particular products or companies to their network.

Open Source Open source is a strategy as much as it is a technology. Open source is a method of distributing software that lets individuals modify code and post it for others to use and benefit by. Linux is an example of open source software that is in direct competition with non-open-source software, such as Microsoft Windows. With the high cost of proprietary software and the difficulty of obtaining support at times, many companies and individuals have turned to open source software for solutions.

PayPal PayPal is a company now owned by eBay that facilitates online payments. First used primarily to handle eBay transactions, it is now used for all sorts of things. Due to its ease of use and security, we recommend it as a way to handle online payments without having to pay credit card merchant fees, and we use it in our own sites regularly. It allows people to send you secure payments, and as a buyer, you have the ability to dispute transactions and follow up. PayPal also has dividend accounts and credit/debit cards that let you access the cash in your account quickly.

Photoblog A photoblog or photolog is photo sharing on a blog. Usually the focus isn't so much on text, as at traditional blogs, but on the photos themselves. YouTube in its current form is more of a videolog, as individuals upload videos, but in "still" format, it would be a photoblog. Interestingly enough, photoblogs have become more common because people have cell phone cameras and therefore fast access to a camera whenever something interesting happens.

Podcast A podcast is media that is sent over the Internet and is downloaded through feeds, mobile devices, RSS, or computers. *Podcasting* is the act of casting your podcast; that is, of submitting your podcast to the public domain on the Internet or the private domain on your intranet.

RSS RSS is a Web feed that updates content in blogs, news feeds, or podcasts. Feed readers are fed by information to which a particular user subscribes. You will want to get your podcast or blog out to RSS feeds so that individuals can subscribe to it and you can build your online reputation.

TypePad TypePad, made by Six Apart Ltd., is one of many blogging services. Check it out at *www.typepad.com.* You may want to use it as your method of submitting blogs.

Uniform Resource Locator (URL) A URL is what you type into a Web browser to get to a particular site. For instance, *http:// drdaniellebabb.com* is the URL to get to one of the coauthors' websites.

Video Blog A video blog or vlog is an entry into a blog that has video or video and text. YouTube became a popular vlog site as individuals from all over the world used their cell phones with cameras to upload video. Everyone became an instant journalist! You can use sites like this to create virtual tours apart from the MLS.

Video Podcasting See *Vodcast.*

Vodcast Video podcasts came about recently as a way to capture podcasts that incorporated video. This is yet another great way to incorporate visual details on your business, your tips, or even your properties.

Web 2.0 *Web 2.0* is an ill-defined term that essentially means "the second version of the Web." This second version of the Web is based on collaboration and interconnectivity, on community and interactivity, and it depends on a community to generate content. It isn't just a push technology; it is a social networking term that collectively describes all of the websites where users have a say in the content.

Web Browser A Web browser is the software that you use to access the Web. For instance, Internet Explorer and FireFox are Web browsers you may use to surf the Internet. Internet Explorer has the largest market share, with Netscape and FireFox behind it. Internet Explorer is integrated into the Windows operating system, which comes on most PCs. The version of the Web browser you use will dictate what you can and cannot see on a Web page, as not all Web programming code displays the same way on all browsers.

Web Server A Web server is the computer or server that takes in HTTP requests from all of its users and then processes them. It may forward a request on to another server, it may handle the request itself, or it may queue the request for later processing. Usually, Web servers work in conjunction with database servers and email servers and do not stand alone to provide Web services, though they can. You will need to buy space on a Web server or have your own Web server (not recommended) to host your site.

Webcast The word *webcast* is part *Web* and part *broadcast*. It means the sending and receiving of video live over the Internet. This is different from a weblog, which can be viewed at any time, or a podcast, which is downloaded later. A webcast is inherently live. Companies use these to deliver annual reports and let their shareholders take part in meetings, for instance.

Webinar A webinar is a seminar that is sent over the Internet; essentially, it is a Web conference. While a webcast is unidirectional—the data is pushed onto the client—a webinar is interactive and synchronous, meaning that the audience participates in real time. Webinars are powerful tools for educating your audience.

Website *Website* is a term that means the entire set of Web pages that make up a domain. For example, all of the Web pages on *www.kaplan.com* together encompass Kaplan's website.

Wiki A wiki is a website that allows visitors to edit the entries in an online interactive encyclopedia. It is a powerful tool to look up definitions and terms.

WordPress WordPress (*http://wordpress.org*) is a blog publishing system that provides a wide toolset to individuals who blog. Some of its tools are free, while others cost money. It is worthwhile to check out for any blogger.

World Wide Web (WWW) The World Wide Web (WWW or Web) is the entire collection of all the hyperlinked sites on the Internet. The WWW excludes email and chat systems; it is everything accessible via your Web browser.

World Wide Web Consortium (W3C) The World Wide Web Consortium (W3C) is an international standards organization that encompasses numerous organizations that work together to develop standards for the Web. It publishes a set of standards that any Web development effort should meet.

YouTube YouTube is a free video-sharing website that lets users upload, review, and share video clips with one another. It has become immensely popular; even major news outlets use video published to it on a regular basis. It was created by three former employees of PayPal and uses Flash to display videos that are uploaded to the site. It was recently purchased by Google and is considered a powerhouse in the world of online entertainment.

Zestimate Zillow.com has coined the term *Zestimate*—a Zillow estimate of home values that is based on a range of publicly available information. A Zestimate includes comps but doesn't take into consideration remodels and upgrades unless you list a house and specifically update it. Many argue that the Zestimate price is not accurate and is fooling sellers into thinking their house is worth more than it is.

Zillow.com Zillow.com is an incredible real estate organization that was started in 2005. Created as an alternative to the MLS, it offers a listing service and a "Make Me Move" service, and it has been widely criticized by the real estate profession. While it has a few kinks to work out, it is becoming immensely popular with consumers.

B Outstanding Websites

THERE ARE LOTS of excellent sites on the Internet. No doubt you frequent them yourself, and many have become household names. Here is a list of many sites that, if you haven't already visited them, we suggest you take the time to do so. We offer the site's name, its address, and a short note about why the site is relevant and important. Happy exploring!

Useful Sites (in random order)

RealTown™
www.realtown.com
The community-generated information on RealTown is second to none in the real estate industry, in our opinions. The site hosts more than 1 million posts on the listserv hosted by InternetCrusade. Two great features of RealTown.com are:

RealTown Blogs

www.realtownblogs.com

The authors use this free, professional blogging service; it is robust, easy to use, and very customizable.

RealTown Communities

www.realtowncommunities.com

RealTown Communities is the part of RealTown designed to share knowledge and strengthen the online community. This is a portal to specific communities with specific purposes. You can create an account and have access to thread watching, signatures, private replies, and subscription management.

Zillow.com

www.zillow.com

Zillow.com, as we mention throughout the book, is a revolutionary company pioneering a new landscape in real estate. This is a can't-miss site for anyone wanting to see what real estate will be in the future!

Domania.com

www.domania.com

Domania is a great site for checking out comparable home prices and valuing homes as well as for searching for new ones. We list this site because it provides a useful tool that many of your clients will be using to benchmark your numbers against.

Google Earth

earth.google.com

This combination of Google's search function and imagery tools lets you view the world in a way your buyers and sellers never imagined!

Wikipedia

www.wikipedia.org

This is the best online encyclopedia we've ever seen! Its user-generated and expert-reviewed content allows you to look up any word and find, not only its meaning, but links to its history and lots of other relevant terms associated with it. It's very powerful—so powerful, in fact, that our glossary section is derived from its definitions and we cite it throughout this book

Podblaze

www.podblaze.com

Podblaze is a full-service podcasting and New Media consulting organization. It lets you create free podcasts and offers much more as well.

PodcastDirectory.com

www.podcastdirectory.com

You can search for podcasts at this site. They also offer news and help on podcasting.

BiggerPockets®

www.biggerpockets.com

Lots of free resources and tools are available at this online real estate guide: discussion forums, services, articles, home value checks, and, of course, real estate blogs.

Real Estate Blog Marketing

www.realestateblogmarketing.com

This company focuses entirely on blog marketing efforts for real estate agents. It helps with lead generation, website search engine visibility, press releases, and other types of marketing.

NameSecure®

www.namesecure.com

Use this site to reserve domain names easily, set up domain email, or forward a new domain name to an existing site if you think of something creative. The authors have used this site for years.

Odeo

www.odeo.com

This site has millions of MP3s and thousands of audio channels, podcasts, music, etc. You can listen, download, and subscribe to this site for free.

Hipcast.com

www.hipcast.com

This audio and video podcasting service allows you to create audio, video, and create and post to blogs.

Gcast

www.gcast.com

This is another great free site that offers hosting, podsafe music (music you can legally use in your podcast), recording by phone, email alerts, and more. This is a must-see and must-browse site if you're new to Web 2.0.

CNET's Download.com

www.download.com

The authors have been using this great site for shareware and freeware from CNET for years. With a quick key word search, you can find lots of great free and low-cost software tools to help do just about anything you can imagine.

WordPress.com

www.wordpress.com

Lots of well-known bloggers use this tool. You can blog on this site for free or use paid upgrades. It offers ways to customize the site, upload photos or images, create sidebars using widgets, create themes, and customize your code. You can also categorize and tag your posts. The tool offers spell checking, previews, auto save features, word saves (it saves it to the server as you type so you never lose more than a minute's worth of data), and tons of privacy options (including member-only blogs). It integrates statistics, has an integrated spam-filtering system, and allows you to import from LiveJournal, TypePad, Blogger, and many other blogs. This organization and tool set is used by a lot of people, so pay close attention to what it offers.

Blogger

www.blogger.com

Owned by Google, Blogger lets you create an account, start a blog, name your blog, create a template, and more. The site is out of beta (test mode) and in full swing. If you are using another blogging service, you can switch fairly painlessly to this one. You can use its Go Mobile feature, post entries, edit, publish, get feedback, and post photos.

Craigslist

www.craigslist.org

This site has become a social phenomenon! Unheard of a few years ago, it is a popular place to list items for sale or wanted. It's like a giant garage sale, only online. Many people list their homes in the real estate section of this site.

MarketingMonday.com

www.marketingmonday.com

This is a marketing site with lots of advice and tips—who can't use that? It has a message board, an audio version, archives, and lots of tools. Some of the advice on marketing in this book is from this site; go here for great information and tools!

The Housing Bubble Blog

www.thehousingbubbleblog.com

We list this site because it won an overall award for blogging and can help you see what an award-winning blog looks like. Notice the option to make donations and the site's content-richness. This site does use a lot of information from other sources. One thing that makes this blog stand out is how incredibly focused it is.

InternetCrusade®

www.internetcrusade.com

This site offers all sorts of opportunities and products that will help you with various aspects of your business, from e-PRO certification courses to technology guides.

Catalist Homes

www.catalisthomes.com

A self-proclaimed home-listing magnet, this is a unique business model that is catching on and causing concern in the traditional real estate market. Check out the site and see what the buzz is about; then take notice and take action! Calling itself a "fat-free broker-age," this site charges a total commission of a mere 3 percent!

Eppraisal.com

www.eppraisal.com

This is an online appraisal site that gives individuals instant information on the value of their homes. This site is in many ways a competitor with Zillow.com. Note that a lot of other sites use the data from here or from Zillow.com to run their own estimates.

For Sale By Owner.com

www.forsalebyowner.com

This site provides resources for individuals who wish to sell their homes on their own (without the aid of a real estate professional). It's important for you to understand the types of sellers that use this site and the types of homes that are listed on it. It's safe to assume that these sellers value technology. How can you incorporate this type of service into your own business?

MySpace.com

www.myspace.com

This is a social-networking website with user-submitted networks of friends. Friends have gone beyond being individuals to being companies, products, or even concepts. Businesses are advertising here, too, by creating a personality for their product or work. MySpace.com is the third most popular website in the United States.

Podcasts in Real Estate—Some Examples

Hopefully by now, you are convinced that podcasts will play a role in your future and in the future of real estate. Take a look at PodcastDirectory.com (*http://podcastdirectory.com*). While there are lots of ads to weed through, you can find a list of podcasts for the real estate industry to get a feel for how they work in your business. BiggerPockets (*www.biggerpockets.com/real-estate-podcasts/*) also hosts a variety of podcasts for the real estate investor to help get your creative ideas flowing. Also, a series of online real estate marketing podcasts for agents is available from Yahoo!; you can watch and download the videos at *http://podcasts.yahoo.com/series?s=b920 4cba4809e4d0443e97c77b149f20*. Even Century 21 has embraced podcasting to provide information to those looking to buy or sell homes, accessible from *www.c21.com/learn/podcast/*.

You may find that podcasts will be useful in marketing. For example, if you do a search for *"real estate"* in Podcast Networks, iTunes, or just about any other directory (even in Google) you will find that homeowners themselves are starting to take advantage of the New Media. There are hundreds of podcasts out there telling homeowners how to take advantage of selling opportunities, how to stage their home, how to hold an open house, and even how to get rid of or mask odors before they let in potential buyers. Others provide insight into the real estate market, the economy in general, how to invest in real estate, and how to value a home. Some companies are turning videos into podcasts for homes for sale. Some podcasts even cater to you, the professional.

Flash Maps

One critical Flash map site for you to look at is USA Real Estate Map (*http://usflashmap.com/products/real_estate_maps/us_flash_map.htm*). Another great site to check out is that of 20/20 DataShed Flexible Inventory and Listings Manager (*http://2020applications.com/listings.asp?itemID=6*).

If you want to get a great website up and going take a look at these sites as well:

- Templatemonster.com (*www.templatemonster.com*)
- Free Site Templates (*http://freesitetemplates.com*)
- Elated Communications (*http://elated.com*)
- TemplatesBox.com (*http://templatesbox.com*)
- Free Layouts.com (*www.freelayouts.com*)
- EasyRealtorPRO (*http://easyrealtorpro.com/site_onlinedemo.php*)

Housing Wire's 2007 Real Estate Blogging Award (REBA)

Housing Wire published the winners of its 2007 REBAs at *www.housingwire.com/2007-rebas/*. The Housing Bubble Blog (*http://thehousingbubbleblog.com*) won the 2007 REBA in the Best Overall category. It never hurts to look at the best of the best! What do you see here that you can use and replicate in your own blog? Why do you think this blog is successful? You can see immediately the "About Me" section. We really like this but don't find it on too many blogs. The blogger gives you a sense of what is important to him and why through his writing, but then he also provides a nice bio front and center. Notice that he asks for donations or at least provides a spot for them. Most people use these donations to fund their research or their writing and writers. Either way, the money usually goes back into the blog. Notice the affiliates to the right? He may or may not be paid for these click-throughs. It does appear that he sells advertising space. He has links on the right and tons of comments in each of his major topics! This is a sign of an active blog.

Winning second place in the Best Overall category was the Mortgage Fraud Blog (*http://mortgagefraudblog.com*). This is a distinctive and purposeful blog. While it isn't as nice to look at, in our opinion, as the first place winner, it is full of great information and insight, and it has the benefit of an attorney's perspective. Notice also the bio located prominently on the page! This is a very busy site with lots of interactivity.

Third place overall was the blog Calculated Risk (*http://calculatedrisk.blogspot.com*). It has an interesting approach with a guest blogger and bios of the site owners under "About CR and Tanta." This is very distinctive and well laid out and looks great; it creates a bit of a tranquil feeling, which is interesting given the content. It uses Google's search features right on the site, and as you'll see, it links to other top blogs, including other award winners. The top dogs have to stick together.

In the Brain Power category, the first place winner was the same as in overall third place: Calculated Risk. Second place in the Brain Power category was Piggington's Econo-Almanac for the Landed Poor (*http://piggington.com*). What struck us about this blog is how local it is. It gave us the feeling of an old newspaper. Also, lots of active forum topics on the right-hand side help educate consumers and can provide great ideas for your own blog.

Third place was Nouriel Roubini's Global Economic Blog (*www. rgemonitor.com/blog/roubini/*). This one, while not our favorite, is interesting in its approach to information—both in terms of its display and content. You can see the RSS button on the right-hand side, something we recommend that everyone have. There is an interesting "Blog Aggregator" link on the left-hand side. Also, note how cleanly the system and menus pop up as one navigates the site, making the site very user-friendly. Note, too, how responsive the site is. While this is really an economics blog and it has some great information and perspective on various economics topics, it maintains relevance to real estate, too.

You can review these blogs for yourself and see what you find most appealing, least appealing, what you may be able to use in your own site, and why others may find them interesting and distinctive.

Many blogs are fantastic but not well known. This is where the REBA's Best-Kept Secret category comes in, though we have a feeling that these sites won't be secret for long! The first place winner in this category was Bubbleinfo.com (*www.bubbleinfo.com*). The second was OC FlipTrack (*www.oc-fliptrack.com*). And the third was the New Jersey Real Estate Report (*http://njrereport.com*).

In the Best Corporate category, the winner was one of our favorites, the Inman Blog from *Inman News* (*http://blog.inman. com*). The second place site was Hot Property from *BusinessWeek* (*http://businessweek.com/the_thread/hotproperty/*). The third place winner, from Bankrate.com and one of Dani's favorite sites for years, was Mortgage Matters (*http://bankrate.com/brm/news/mortgages/ mortgage_update.asp*).

In the Best Regional category, the winner was the Vancouver Housing Market Blog (*http://van-housing.blogspot.com*). Note which hosting service they are using! The second place blog was the Sacramento Land(ing) (*http://sacramentolanding.blogspot.com*). Third place was the New Jersey Real Estate Report (*http://njrereport. com*). Most likely this local category is one in which you will be able to work well, and our research shows that it will be most useful to building your brand and your reputation as a local expert. Pay careful attention to these local winners and see what they do well and what you could improve on in your own blog.

In the Most Extreme category, the winner was HousingPANIC (*http://housingpanic.blogspot.com*). Second place was Another FB (*http://housingbubblecasualty.com*). Third place was The Housing Bubble Blog (*http://thehousingbubbleblog.com*), which you'll note also won first place overall.

Some real estate pros are using how-to blogs to educate the consumer and be seen as a friend rather than foe to the educated buyer or seller. The How-To category winner was The Real Estate Tomato (*http://realestatetomato.typepad.com*). Second place was one of our favorites, Realty Blogging (*www.realtyblogging.com*). Third place was Future of Real Estate Marketing (*http://futureofrealestatemarketing. com*). We recommend that you invest a considerable amount of time and sit down with each of these blogs. Take note of what you like, what you don't like, what you think needs to be improved, what is already done well, what is of value, what isn't, and what look and feel the site has—what personality does it convey? What components of the site convey personality? Is it all in the writing, or is there more to it?

Our Reviews of Some Existing Agent Sites

The Web is full of real estate agent websites that run the gamut from amateurish to "wow!" Probably the best way to illustrate our advice on what makes a good website is to direct you to some existing ones and let you know what we think of them. Below are ten sites that we have scoured the Internet to find. We feel that each of them is typical in its own way and that, together, they provide an accurate representation of real estate agent sites on the Internet. In other words, after you check out all ten, you'll have a good idea of the types of sites that are out there.

We rate each site according to four elements: content, appearance, "cutting-edginess," and usability. The content element simply refers to the actual contents of the site, with consideration for the relevance of the material. Keep in mind that more content does not necessarily make the website better. In fact, too much content is distracting and detrimental. The appearance element refers to the look and feel of the site. The usability element has to do with ease of use and navigation. The cutting-edginess element is related to the degree of inclusion of the latest Web technologies.

Each element is assigned a grade, from A+ at the upper end to F at the lower end. We also include a fifth element, which corresponds to an overall grade that considers the first four elements. Finally, we have a sixth element, which is a ranking of each site in relation to the other nine, with the best site being 1 and the worst 10. Please keep in mind that these sites were reviewed when this book was written; by the time the book goes to print, it is quite possible for any of them to have gone through a major renovation.

Title: Lang Vermont Real Estate is now Lang McLaughry Spera—the largest Vermont real estate firm serving Vermont and Northern New Hampshire.

URL: *http://langrealestate.com*

Review: This is the website of a conglomerate of three real estate firms, Lang Associates, McLaughry Real Estate, and Pall Spera Company, who all recently merged. The newly created firm specializes in properties in Vermont and northern New Hampshire. Overall, this is one of the best websites we have seen. This is probably due to the fact that there is much more than a small operation behind it, but even a single agent can have an equally impressive site. Among other things, this website features the LMS TV Show, which is basically just that; a television-quality podcast that showcases the firm's various listings. In addition, there is a link to an active blog, Vermont Buzz, that contains quite a bit of useful information.

(1) Content Grade:		A
(2) Appearance Grade:		A
(3) Usability Grade:		A
(4) Cutting-Edginess Grade:		A+
(5) Overall Grade:		A
(6) Overall Ranking:		1/10

Title: The Real Estate Blog

URL: *http://franandrowena.blogspot.com*

Review: This is the blog website of Fran and Rowena (would you believe that they don't list their last names anywhere?) who specialize in the Pasadena, California, area. This blog is certainly top-notch and worth checking out. The topics are relevant and up to date. However, the association with Fran and Rowena is a bit weak. This may be due to the limitations of the blog platform, but it certainly is a weakness. It's a shame to have such a nice blog but with very little credit attributed to its authors.

(1)	Content Grade:	A
(2)	Appearance Grade:	A–
(3)	Usability Grade:	A
(4)	Cutting-Edginess Grade:	A
(5)	Overall Grade:	A
(6)	Overall Ranking:	2/10

Title: Find Real Estate services in Montgomery, AL

URL: *http://www.homesforsaleinmontgomeryalabama.com*

Review: This is a site for a real estate agent by the name of Sandra Nickel who works in Montgomery, Alabama. It is designed in a very user-friendly yet attractive manner. In addition to providing useful information on her and her team, it incorporates all the tools and resources that a potential client would want. Best of all, it contains a link to her podcast site which is hosted by Talk Realty. Her podcast library is extensive, up to date, and relevant. Ms. Nickel's website is a wonderful example of what a typical real estate agent can accomplish. What's most impressive is that she's not a part of any of the large real estate brokerages, yet the presentation of her website certainly portrays her as "big time." When looking at it, put yourself in the place of a potential client; you'll be able to appreciate the impression that it leaves on you. The only negative that we can come up with is the lengthy (yet somehow memorable) URL.

(1)	Content Grade:	A
(2)	Appearance Grade:	A–
(3)	Usability Grade:	A
(4)	Cutting-Edginess Grade:	B+
(5)	Overall Grade:	A–
(6)	Overall Ranking:	3/10

Title: Toni Haber | Upper West Side Upper East Side Chelsea Real Estate New York Real Estate & New York City Real Estate

URL: *http://tonihaber.com*

Review: This is the website of Toni Haber, a real estate agent who focuses on mid- to high-end properties in New York. The title is overkill in terms of length, but this site is exceptional in that so much information is compacted into a relatively small area, yet it is done in an organized manner. Everything you would want to know about Haber and her properties can be found on the site. There is even an informative blog, but unfortunately it is a bit hidden, as the link to it is part of the very small print at the bottom of the page. This website provides Haber with instant credibility.

(1)	Content Grade:	A
(2)	Appearance Grade:	A–
(3)	Usability Grade:	A–
(4)	Cutting-Edginess Grade:	A–
(5)	Overall Grade:	A–
(6)	Overall Ranking:	4/10

Title: John McMonigle | McMonigle Group—Newport Beach Real Estate

URL: *http://mcmoniglegroup.com*

Review: This is the website of John McMonigle, a real estate agent based in Orange County, California. Mr. McMonigle deals with high-end properties in the luxurious coastal communities of Orange County. He was recently featured on an episode of Oprah in which he showcased a $75 million listing called The Portabello Estate. The site is impressive but a bit intimidating. If a potential homebuyer's budget is not in the several-million-dollar range, not much there would be useful. Mr. McMonigle's target market is the superrich, but why not use the power of the Web to attract all types of buyers, even if you end up referring them to others? This is an example of a website that's designed more for show than to garner business.

(1)	Content Grade:	C+
(2)	Appearance Grade:	A–
(3)	Usability Grade:	B+
(4)	Cutting-Edginess Grade:	B+
(5)	Overall Grade:	B
(6)	Overall Ranking:	5/10

Title: Naples Florida Real Estate, Pelican Bay Real Estate

URL: *www.staciericci.com*

Review: This is the website of Stacie Ricci, a real estate agent in Naples, Florida, who focuses on all types of properties. This is a great example of a simple yet effective website. This is not the type of website we've been highlighting throughout the book, because it lacks much of the functionality of Web v2, but it can be considered appropriate for the service that Ricci is offering and for her clientele. If your website is similar to this one, we would certainly recommend that you spice it up a bit by implementing a blog and a podcast. Why be run of the mill when you can be exceptional?

(1) Content Grade:		B–
(2) Appearance Grade:		B–
(3) Usability Grade:		B
(4) Cutting-Edginess Grade:		C
(5) Overall Grade:		B–
(6) Overall Ranking:		6/10

Title: Lake Havasu City Arizona—Lake Havasu City Homes and Real Estate For Sale—REALTOR®

URL: *www.forsalebysandy.com*

Review: This is the website of Sandy Norman, a real estate agent servicing the area of Lake Havasu City, Arizona. Norman has decided to let the area she services be just as much the focus of her site as she and her services. In contrast to Toni Haber's home page, Sandy Norman's is quite long. In other words, a visitor to the site would have to do quite a bit of vertical scrolling to see all the content. Do you see the difference between the two? We feel that Norman's site has too much information on the main page. We highly doubt that anyone will read all of it, and much of it should have been filed elsewhere. With regard to her picture, it's about halfway down the page (you have to scroll down to see it), which makes it appear as if she is almost secondary. This is not good—she should be the focus. In addition, the picture should be incorporated better into the background of the page. On the bright side, the "My Listings" section is simple and effective.

(1)	Content Grade:	C+
(2)	Appearance Grade:	B
(3)	Usability Grade:	B–
(4)	Cutting-Edginess Grade:	C+
(5)	Overall Grade:	B–
(6)	Overall Ranking:	7/10

Title: Charlottesville Real Estate (Charles 434-981-1585) Charlottesville VA Real Estate, Homes, Land

URL: *http://mycharlottesvilleagent.com*

Review: If you'd like an example of a website design that you should *not* emulate under any circumstances, look no further than the website of Charles McDonald. McDonald is a real estate agent specializing in Charlottesville, Virginia. The amount of information, the way that information is presented, and the number of colors involved are all way off what we would consider acceptable. We are willing to bet our entire proceeds from this book that not one person has ever gone through all the information found on the home page. This website appears as if it is designed to confuse. The only redeeming quality is the blog, which is quite nice, but this is because it is designed in a completely different manner than the rest of the site. McDonald would be well served by cutting back drastically on the "in your face" theme of his website and instead giving his blog a bit more focus.

(1)	Content Grade:	B
(2)	Appearance Grade:	D
(3)	Usability Grade:	C–
(4)	Cutting-Edginess Grade:	B
(5)	Overall Grade:	C+
(6)	Overall Ranking:	8/10

Title: Newton Real Estate, Wellesley Real Estate, Homes For Sale, Condos, Relocation Realtors MA

URL: *http://homesbynorcross.com*

Review: This is the website of Christine Norcross, a real estate agent who specializes in homes located in an area within Boston, Massachusetts. The first thing that sticks out about this site is that Norcross's picture is nowhere to be found on the main page. In fact, it almost appears as if she is an afterthought. Remember, your website is about *you*. Your website needs to say with authority, "This is who I am, and this is what I can do for you!" rather than whispering something to the effect of "Here's some information about the area. Let me know if I can be of any assistance." Passiveness will not get you very far today, given all the competing sites out there.

(1) Content Grade:		C
(2) Appearance Grade:		C–
(3) Usability Grade:		C
(4) Cutting-Edginess Grade:		C–
(5) Overall Grade:		C–
(6) Overall Ranking:		9/10

Title: Welcome—Christine Brody—Real Estate Virginia Beach Homes Realtor

URL: *www.realtorvabeach.com*

Review: This is the website of Christine Brody, a real estate agent focusing on the Virginia Beach, Virginia, area. At first glance, the site appears quite bland. The overuse of grays is not eye-catching at all. The size of the graphical links on the left-hand side (e.g., "About Me" and "Client Testimonials") is quite small, making them difficult to read. This is not a site that will go very far in terms of attracting new clients. At the time we viewed this site, Ms. Brody had only a single listing (a townhome) on the "My Listings" page. If you were a potential client, what message would this send?

(1)	Content Grade:	C
(2)	Appearance Grade:	D
(3)	Usability Grade:	C+
(4)	Cutting-Edginess Grade:	D+
(5)	Overall Grade:	D+
(6)	Overall Ranking:	10/10

General Tools

To help create a sense of community, consider the free tool called Joomla!. It is open source, meaning that the code can be modified and does not cost anything. Though not all of the modules are open source (such as the one for real estate), they are very inexpensive. Developers create themes for these sites that are W3C compliant (we talked about this in Chapter 5), so you can really create a great website that is multibrowser compliant for very little cost. Check out *http://joomla.com* and the real estate module at *http://mosets.com/hotproperty/modules/*. If you want to include a magazine, check out iJoomla.com (*www.ijoomla.com*) or an example at *www.chattanoogacity.com*. Property reviews that the general public can see (perhaps including seller or agent ratings like those given to eBay users) are another feature to consider, and Joomla! has modules for that as well at *http://demo.reviewsforjoomla.com*. Additional themes can be downloaded from JoomlArt.com (*www. joomlart.com/index.php*). The goal here is to get familiar with open source content management system (CMS) software. Also, take a look at Open-Realty® (*http://open-realty.org*), a system that is specific to real estate. And be sure to ask your developer about XOOPS, a dynamic CMS that includes modules that can benefit a real estate site.

Acknowledgments

To Matt—thanks for putting up with my crazy schedule.

To my gramps—another one for your coffee table!

To my parents—no, you don't have to buy it at a retailer!

To my bro and nephew—you bring a lot of happiness to my life.

To Bob Diforio, our agent—what can I say besides "you rock"?

To the Real Town team—for doing what they do so well!

To my bud and coauthor—we've laughed, yelled, and schemed; I couldn't ask for a better friend!

To Cheryl Ann Henry, for her insight and her excellent advice to our readers!

—DANI BABB

Things have been really hectic for me the last few years, and my wife has done a wonderful job handling everything. With all the changes that have gone on in our lives, she has adjusted wonderfully.

—ALEX LAZO

References

Babb, D. 2006. *Commissions at risk: A real estate professional's guide to beating online competition.* New York: Kaplan.

BiggerPockets. 2006. Retrieved from *http://biggerpockets.com/real-estate-podcasts/*.

Catalist Homes. 2003. Retrieved from *http://catalisthomes.com/aboutMission.aspx*.

Decrem, B. 2006. Introducing Flock Beta 1. Retrieved from *http://flock.com/node/4500*.

Eamer, M. 2007. Blogging SEO and syndication. Retrieved from *http://zillowblog.com/zillow_blog/2007/02/blogging_seo_an.html*.

Evans, B. 2003. Generation gap: X marks the spot. Retrieved from *www.realtor.org/rmoprint.nsf/pages/BEvans200301272*.

Gibbons, D. 2007. Attracting a conversation: Blog comment tips. Retrieved from *http://zillowblog.com/zillow_blog/2007/02/blog_comments.html*.

Haddad, A. 2005. Low-priced brokerage is shaking up real estate. Retrieved from the Internet at *http://www.latimes.com/business/la-fi-catalist1dec01,0,5996032.story*.

Hagerty, J. 2005. Discount real-estate brokers spark a war over commissions. Retrieved from *www.realestatejournal.com/buysell/markettrends/20051013-hagerty.html*.

Heller, F. 2006. Podcasting's impact on real estate. Retrieved from *www.realtor.org/rmomag.NSF/pages/techwatch2006022?Open Document.*

Helmering, J. 2006. Real estate podcasting. Retrieved from *www. realestateblogsites.com/public/item/124683.*

Henry, C. 2006. Personal interview with Web architect by the authors.

HomeRoute Real Estate Services. 2007. eMarketing quiz. Retrieved from *www.homeroute.com/marketing-quiz/.*

Housely, S. n.d. Set your podcast up for success. Retrieved from *http://feedforall.com/podcasting-tips.htm.*

Housing Wire. 2007. Retrieved from *www.housingwire.com/ 2007/01/15/announcing-the-2007-reba-winners/.*

Inman News. 2006. What the Zillow announcement means. Retrieved from *www.inman.com/inmannews.aspx?ID=59838.*

Klein, S. 2006. 10 Blog Tips. Retrieved from *http://saul. realtownblogs.com/publishing/.*

Kruse, R. 2006. The power of email. Retrieved from *http:// activerain.com/blogsview/The-Power-of-Email?9210.*

Lavery, L. 2007. Avoiding legal pitfalls in blogging. Retrieved from *http://zillowblog.com/zillow_blog/2007/01/avoiding_legal_.html.*

Lockwood, J. 2007. 7 myths about real estate blogging. Retrieved from *http://realestatetomato.typepad.com/the_real_estate_ tomato/2007/02/7_myths_about_r.html.*

Losh, J. B. Luxury homebuyers like agents with websites. 2005. Retrieved from *http://realtytimes.com/rtapages/20050721_ luxuryhomes.htm.*

Macintosh, R. n.d. Marketing & promotion: Domain names. Retrived from *http://www.designstop.com/marketing-promotion/ domain-names/domains.htm.*

MarketingMonday.com 2006. How to sell more of your own listings for more money, in less time in any market. Retrieved from *http://marketingmonday.com/archives/013.html*.

Meyers, D. 2007. Content is king, but the voice is queen. Retrieved from *http://zillowblog.com/zillow_blog/2007/01/content_is_king.html*.

National Association of REALTORS®. *http://www.realtor.org*.

Nielsen (2005). Ratings Research. Retrieved from *http://allabout marketresearch.com*.

Newton, J. *Los Gatos Weekly Times*. 2005. Home sales increase: So does the number of agents. Retrieved from *www.community-newspapers.com/archives/lgwt/20050921/lg-re-feature2.shtml*.

Nordwall, B. 2007. Setting up your blog. Retrieved from *http://zillowblog.com/zillow_blog/2007/01/setting_up_your.html*.

O'Reilly, T. What is Web 2.0: Design patterns and business models for the next generation of software. Retrieved from *http://oreillynet.com/pub/a/oreilly/tim/news/2005/09/30/what-is-Web-20.html*.

Ravens, D. 2006. eMarketing 101: Chapter 1; What is emarketing and how is it better than traditional marketing. Retrieved from *http://ezinearticles.com/?eMarketing-101—Chapter-1:-What-is-eMarketing-and-How-is-it-Better-Than-Traditional-Marketing &id=364179*.

Real estate journal home price check. 2006. Retrieved from *http://realestatejournal.domania.com/homepricecheck/index.jsp*.

Series information: Online real estate marketing podcast for agents. 2006. Retrieved from *http://podcasts.yahoo.com/series?s=b9204cba4809e4d0443e97c77b149f20*.

Sullivan, D. 2007. How to use HTML meta tags. Retrieved from *http://searchenginewatch.com/showPage.html?page=2167931*.

Index

About the Authors

Danielle Babb, PhD, MBA

Danielle Babb is a technology professional with years of experience in the real estate industry. She has worked as an IT leader in residential, commercial, and multiunit real estate. She has worked for seven years at several *Fortune* 500 real estate companies in the technology field and both consults and presents regularly on the use of technology in real estate. She is the author of the book *Commissions at Risk,* which gives professionals the inside scoop on what to expect in the real estate industry in the future. Danielle has a PhD in organization and management with a technology emphasis as well as an MBA with a technology emphasis. She has written and presented numerous papers on technology and business and has become a specialist in the field of technology's impact on business. Dani is a California Licensed Real Estate Professional.

Alex Lazo, PhD, MS

Alex Lazo has worked in the information technology field for over 20 years, with much of that time spent in the real estate industry. Alex has a PhD in organization and management with a technology emphasis, as well as a master's degree in management information systems. As an avid longtime real estate investor, Alex has been able to incorporate his vast knowledge of technology into his real estate ventures. He has experience in both residential and commercial real estate and has managed all aspects of technology in this business.

With products serving children, adults, schools and businesses, Kaplan has an educational solution for every phase of learning.

SCORE! Educational Centers offer individualized tutoring programs in reading, math, writing and other subjects for students ages 4-14 at more than 160 locations across the country. We help students achieve their academic potential while developing self-confidence and a love of learning. ***www.escore.com***

We also partner with schools and school districts through Kaplan K12 Learning Services to provide instructional programs that improve results and help all students achieve. We support educators with professional development, innovative technologies, and core and supplemental curriculum to meet state standards. ***www.kaplank12.com***

Kaplan Test Prep and Admissions prepares students for more than 80 standardized tests, including entrance exams for secondary school, college and graduate school, as well as English language and professional licensing exams. We also offer private tutoring and one-on-one admissions guidance. ***www.kaptest.com***

Kaplan Higher Education offers postsecondary programs in fields such as business, criminal justice, health care, education, and information technology through more than 70 campuses in the U.S. and abroad, as well as online programs through Kaplan University and Concord Law School.
www.khec.com
www.kaplan.edu
www.concordlawschool.edu

If you are looking to start a new career or advance in your field, Kaplan Professional offers training to obtain and maintain professional licenses and designations in the accounting, financial services, real estate and technology industries. We also work with businesses to develop solutions to satisfy regulatory mandates for tracking and compliance. ***www.kaplanprofessional.com***

Kaplan helps individuals achieve their educational and career goals.
We build futures one success story at a time.